LATIN
Everywhere, Everyday

Teacher's Manual

Elizabeth Heimbach

Bolchazy-Carducci Publishers, Inc.
Wauconda, Illinois USA

Editor
LeaAnn A. Osburn

Typography and Cover Design
Adam Phillip Velez

**Latin Everywhere, Everyday
Teacher's Manual**

Elizabeth Heimbach

Audio CD
James Chochola

Printed in the United States of America
2005
by United Graphics

BOLCHAZY-CARDUCCI PUBLISHERS, INC.
1000 Brown Street, Unit 101
Wauconda, Illinois 60084 U.S.A.
www.bolchazy.com

ISBN: 0-86516-589-0

CONTENTS

CHAPTER ONE

Answers to Chapter One

Sententiae Latinae

Exercises, p. 3

I. Write the English meaning for each Latin expression:

    1.   ab ovo usque ad mala   from eggs to apples, from beginning to end

    2.   ab ovo   from the egg, from the beginning

    3.   ab initio   from the beginning

    4.   ad hoc   to this, for this purpose

    5.   ad hominem   to the man, personal

    6.   ad infinitum   to the infinite, endlessly

II. Fill in the blank with the Latin expression that is translated in the parentheses:

    1.   Our town has formed an *ad hoc* **(for this purpose)** committee to look into the issue of recycling.

    2.   The group will consider the present program *ab ovo*, or *ab initio* **(from the beginning)**.

    3.   Then, the committee will redesign the program *ab ovo usque ad malo* **(from beginning to end)**.

    4.   One of the members of the new committee has a reputation for talking *ad infinitum* **(endlessly)**, but no one will make an *ad hominem* **(personal)** attack on him.

Exercises, p. 5

I. Write the English meaning for each Latin expression:

1. ad libitum (ad lib.)   at pleasure, without preparation

2. ad nauseam   to seasickness, to the point of disgust

3. alibi   elsewhere, defense of being elsewhere when a crime was committed

4. alma mater   nourishing mother, school or college attended or school song

5. alumnus, alumna   foster child, graduate of a school or college

II. Review all the Latin expressions you have learned. Then match each expression with its English meaning:

1. __J__ ab ovo usque ad mala   A. elsewhere

2. __A__ alibi   B. without preparation

3. __D__ ad hoc   C. from the beginning

4. __H__ ad hominem   D. for this purpose

5. __G__ ad infinitum   E. graduate of a school

6. __E__ alumnus, alumna   F. nourishing mother

7. __B__ ad lib.   G. endlessly

8. __F__ alma mater   H. personal

9. __I__ ad nauseam   I. to the point of disgust

10. __C__ ab initio   J. from beginning to end

Exercises, p. 7

I.   Write the English meaning for each Latin expression:

    1.   alter ego   another self, perfect substitute or deputy

    2.   amicus curiae   friend of the court, a person who advises the court on a matter before it

    3.   annuit coeptis   He (God) has nodded at (our) undertakings, He (God) has favored (our) undertakings

    4.   anno Domini (A.D.)   in the year of the Lord, Common Era

    5.   ante bellum   before the war, before the American Civil War

II.   Answer briefly:

    1.   During what period of American history did Eli Whitney invent the cotton gin?
           The *antebellum* period

    2.   Who was Dr. Jeckyll's *alter ego*?
           Mr. Hyde

    3.   What is another way to write the date 79 CE?
           A.D. 79

    4.   Why would someone submit an *amicus curiae* brief to a court?
           To give the judge information

    5.   Where would you find the words, *annuit coeptis* on the dollar bill? What other Latin phrases can you find?
           Above the pyramid on the back are the words *novus ordo seclorum* (new world order) and *e pluribus unum* (out of many one).

III.   Write English sentences to show that you know the meaning of "amicable" and "belligerent." Some sample sentences are below.

    1.   After the dispute, the quarrelsome neighbors came to an amicable agreement.
    2.   The bully clenched his fists in a belligerent way.

Exercises, p. 9

I. Write the English meaning for each Latin expression:

    1.   ante meridiem (A.M.)   before noon, in the morning

    2.   arma virumque cano   I sing of arms and the man, I tell of wars and a hero

    3.   ars gratia artis   art for the sake of art

    4.   ars longa, vita brevis   art (is) long, life (is) short

    5.   ave atque vale   hail and farewell, hello and goodbye

II. How many Latin words do you remember?

    1.   ante   before

    2.   vita   life

    3.   brevis   short

    4.   longa   long

    5.   virum   man

III. Give the meaning of each English word:

    1.   virile = manly

    2.   vital = of, pertaining to, or necessary to life

    3.   abbreviate = shorten

    4.   valedictorian = a student, usually with the highest academic rank, who gives a farewell address

    5.   vitamin = any of a group of organic substances essential in small quantities to metabolism

Exercises, p. 11

I.   Write the English meaning for each Latin expression:

1.   bona fide   in good faith, genuine

2.   calvo turpius est   nothing (is) uglier than a bald (man) with hair
     nihil comato

3.   carpe diem   seize the day, enjoy today

4.   casus belli   cause of war

5.   cave canem   beware of the dog

II. Unscramble these Latin words:

1.   perac mied = *carpe diem*

2.   abno edif = *bona fide*

3.   menac acev = *cave canem*

4.   libel ssuac = *casus belli*

III. Draw a sketch of someone about whom you might say, *"Calvo turpius est nihil comato!"*
     A sample sketch is below.

Exercises, p. 13

I.   Write the English meaning for each Latin expression:

    1.   caveat emptor   let the buyer beware

    2.   circa (ca., c.)   around, approximately

    3.   cogito ergo sum   I think, therefore I am

    4.   confer (cf.)   compare

    5.   cornucopia   horn of plenty

II.   How many abbreviations do you remember? Give **the Latin words** and the **English meaning** for each:

		Latin Words	English Meaning
1.	ad lib.	*ad libitum*	at pleasure, without preparation
2.	A.D.	*anno Domini*	in the year of the Lord, Common Era
3.	A.M.	*ante meridiem*	before noon, in the morning
4.	ca., c.	*circa*	around, approximately
5.	cf.	*confer*	compare

III. What do each of these English words mean:

    1.   emporium = a store

    2.   caveat = a warning

Exercises, p. 15

I. Write the English meaning for each Latin expression:

1. corpus delicti   the body of an offense, the basic element of a crime

2. credo   I believe, a set of firm beliefs

3. cui bono   to whom for a good, to whose advantage, for whose benefit

4. cum grano salis   with a grain of salt, with a little disbelief, not too seriously

5. cum laude   with praise, with honor

II. Review expressions 25–35. Then match each expression with its English meaning:

1. C   cave canem   A. compare

2. B   caveat emptor   B. let the buyer beware

3. D   circa (ca., c.)   C. beware of the dog

4. J   cogito ergo sum   D. approximately

5. A   confer (cf.)   E. set of beliefs

6. H   corpus delicti   F. with praise, honor

7. E   credo   G. with a little disbelief

8. I   cui bono   H. body of an offense

9. G   cum grano salis   I. to whose advantage

10. F   cum laude   J. I think, therefore I am

Exercises, p. 17

I. Write the English meaning for each Latin expression:

1. curriculum vitae   lap of life, resume, summary of one's career

2. de facto   from the fact, in fact, in reality

3. de jure   from law, by law

4. de gustibus non est disputandum   concerning tastes there is to be no dispute, there is no accounting for tastes

5. de minimis non curat lex   the law does not care about the smallest things, the law is not concerned with trifles

II. Use your knowledge of Latin to find the best meaning for these English words:

1. jurisprudence
    a. the science and philosophy of medicine
    b. the science and philosophy of architecture
    c. the science and philosophy of law

2. gustatory
    a. disgusting
    b. tasteless
    c. having to do with taste

3. minimal
    a. least
    b. most
    c. major

4. curricle
    a. part of a fingernail
    b. a small horse drawn carriage
    c. contamination

5. disputatious
    a. argumentative
    b. tasteless
    c. legal

Exercises, p. 19

I.   Write the English meaning for each Latin expression:

1.	de mortuis nil nisi bonum	about the dead (say) nothing except good
2.	de novo	from the new, anew
3.	deus ex machina	god from the machine, any artificial or improbable device used to resolve the difficulties of a plot
4.	docendo discitur	one learns by teaching
5.	dramatis personae	the masks of a drama, (cast of) characters in a play

II. Write an English word that is related to each of these Latin words. Some sample answers are below.

1.	discitur	(1) discipline = training to act in accordance with rules, drill (2) disciple = one who assists in spreading the teachings of another
2.	mortuis	mortal = human being
3.	docendo	docent = guide
4.	novo	novice = beginner

III. Pick three of the expressions from numbers 41–45, and use each in an English sentence that shows the meaning. Some sample sentences are below.

1.   *De mortuis nil nisi bonum* is the motto of the reporter who writes obituaries.

2.   Let's begin the discussion *de novo.*

3.   Eliot's novel, *The Mill on the Floss,* ends with a *deus ex machina,* when a flood drowns everyone

4.   The new teacher often said, *"Docendo discitur."*

5.   When I go to see a play, I always read the list of the *dramatis personae* in my theater program.

Exercises, p. 21

I. Write the English meaning for each Latin expression:

1. dulce et decorum est
    pro patria mori

    it is sweet and fitting to die for one's country

2. e pluribus unum

    out of many (ingredients) one (stew),
    out of many (backgrounds/states) one (nation)

3. emeritus, emerita

    with merit, retired

4. errare humanum est

    to err is human, everybody makes mistakes

5. et alia (et al.)

    and the others

II. Use your knowledge of Latin to figure out what each English word means. Then, check a dictionary. Write the correct definition and an English sentence showing that you understand the meaning of each word. Some sample definitions and sentences are below.

1. dulcimer = a modern folk instrument with three or four strings plucked or strummed with the fingers
    The concert ended with a musician playing a dulcimer and singing a sad song.

2. erratum (pl. errata) = an error in writing or printing
    The errata are found at the end of the article.

3. pluralistic = characteristic of a society in which minority groups participate fully in the dominant society yet maintain their cultural differences.
    The United States has a pluralistic culture.

4. expatriate = dwelling in a foreign land; exiled
    The American expatriates celebrated Thanksgiving together.

5. decorum = the customs and observances of polite society
    Everyone behaved with decorum at the formal dinner.

Exercises, p. 23

I.   Write the English meaning for each Latin expression:

    1.   et cetera (etc.)   and the rest

    2.   et tu, Brute?   Also you, Brutus? Even you, Brutus?

    3.   ex cathedra   from (the bishop's) chair, with authority

    4.   ex libris   from the books, from the library (of)

    5.   ex nihilo nihil fit   Nothing is made from nothing.

II. Use the Latin you have learned to translate the following words:
(Hint: some of these words are from expressions you learned earlier.)

    1.   ex   from, out of

    2.   et   and, also, even

    3.   tu   you

    4.   cum   with

    5.   nihil   nothing

    6.   ego   I

    7.   vita   life

    8.   lex   law

    9.   est   is

    10.   bellum   war

Exercises, p. 25

I.   Write the English meaning for each Latin expression:

1.   ex officio   from the office, by virtue of one's position

2.   ex post facto   from what is done afterward, retroactively, subsequently

3.   ex tempore   out of the time, at the moment, on the spur of the moment

4.   exempli gratia (e.g.)   for the sake of an example, for example

5.   exeat   let him/her leave, a permission to leave

II. Look over the abbreviations you have learned from 36–60. Give the Latin and the English for each:

1.   e.g.   *exempli gratia*   for example, for the sake of an example

2.   C.V.   *curriculum vitae*   resume, summary of one's life

3.   et al.   *et alia*   and the others

4.   etc.   *et cetera*   and the rest

5.   ca., c.   *circa*   around, approximately

6.   cf.   *confer*   compare

III. Use one of the abbreviations in exercise II in a sentence which shows you know its meaning. Some sample sentences are below.

1.   Many great movies, e.g., *Return of the King,* are based on books.
2.   To apply for the job you must submit your C.V.
3.   The book's authors are listed as Smith, Jones, et al.
4.   Pack your toothbrush, pajamas, etc. for the overnight.
5.   Many exciting discoveries characterize the fifteenth century, ca. 1492.
6.   The article about Charlotte Bronte's unusual childhood ended with the reference, cf. Emily and Anne Bronte.

Exercises, p. 27

I.   Write the English meaning for each Latin expression:

    1.   exit   he/she leaves, way out

    2.   exeunt omnes   they all leave

    3.   festina lente   make haste slowly

    4.   fiat lux   let there be light, let light be made

    5.   finis   the end

II. Match:

    1.   <u>B</u>   fiat lux   A.   hurry slowly

    2.   <u>A</u>   festina lente   B.   let there be light, let light be made

    3.   <u>E</u>   exit   C.   the end

    4.   <u>C</u>   finis   D.   they all leave

    5.   <u>D</u>   exeunt omnes   E.   way out

III. Find out three facts about the Roman emperor Augustus, whose motto was *festina lente*. List them below. Some sample answers are below.

    1.   Augustus' real name was Octavius. His dates are 63 BCE–14 CE.

    2.   Augustus was the great nephew and adopted son of Julius Caesar.

    3.   Augustus' wife was named Livia, and his daughter was named Julia.

    4.   The month of August was named in Augustus' honor.

Exercises, p. 29

I.   Write the English meaning for each Latin expression:

    1.   genius loci   guardian spirit of a place

    2.   habeas corpus   may you have the body (of evidence), right of citizens to avoid unlawful imprisonment

    3.   homo sapiens   wise human, human being

    4.   ibidem (ibid.)   in the same place

    5.   id est (i.e.)   that is, in other words

II. Connect the beginning of each expression to its missing part (hint: some of the expressions are from 60–70):

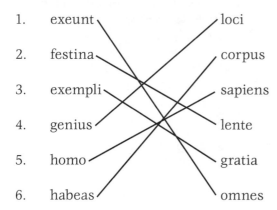

    1.   exeunt   loci

    2.   festina   corpus

    3.   exempli   sapiens

    4.   genius   lente

    5.   homo   gratia

    6.   habeas   omnes

III. Circle the best meaning for each English word:

    1.   sapient   A.   **wise**
                                   B.   saline
                                   C.   stupid

    2.   deity   A.   **god**
                                   B.   priest
                                   C.   genius

    3.   hominid   A.   **related to a human**
                                   B.   homely
                                   C.   small insect

Exercises, p. 31

I.   Write the English meaning for each Latin expression:

     1.   ignis fatuus   foolish fire, something misleading, will-o'-the-wisp

     2.   ignoramus   we are ignorant, an extremely ignorant person

     3.   ignorantia legis   ignorance of the law excuses no one
             neminem excusat

     4.   in absentia   in one's absence

     5.   in extremis   among the last things, in extreme circumstances, at the point of death

II. Write the definition of each English word. Then write the Latin word from which each English word is derived. Some sample definitions are below.

     1.   fatuous   foolish
                                  fatuus

     2.   ignite   set on fire
                                  ignis

     3.   extreme   intense
                                  extremis

III. Fill in the blank with the Latin expression that is translated in the parentheses:

     1.   When it comes to spelling I am an *ignoramus* (**an extremely ignorant person**).

     2.   The *ignis fatuus* (**will-o'-the-wisp**) proved to be nothing more than moonlight reflected in the puddle.

     3.   The drowning swimmer cried out for help when he was *in extremis* (**at the point of death**).

     4.   My friend was not at the meeting so she was elected secretary of the group *in absentia* (**in absence).**

Exercises, p. 33

I. Write the English meaning for each Latin expression:

1. in flagrante delicto   in a burning crime, caught red handed, caught in the act

2. in hoc signo vinces   in this sign you will conquer

3. in loco parentis   in place of a parent

4. in medias res   into the midst of things

5. in memoriam   in memory

II. Answer briefly. Some sample answers are below.

1. What is the Latin root of the English word "flagrant?" What does the Latin word mean? What does "flagrant" mean?
    flagrante = burning
    flagrant = shockingly noticeable

2. What kind of ancient literature begins *in medias res?* Give an example.
    epic
    The *Iliad*, the *Odyssey*, the *Aeneid*

3. In what section of a newspaper would you find the phrase *in memoriam?*
    the obituaries

4. Where did Maxentius and Constantine fight a decisive battle for control of the Roman Empire?
    The Milvian Bridge

5. What sign did Constantine see the night before the battle with Maxentius?
    ☧ = Chi Rho

Exercises, p. 35

I.   Write the English meaning for each Latin expression:

1.   in re   in the matter (of)

2.   in situ   in place, in its original position

3.   in toto   in total, entirely

4.   in utero   in the womb, unborn

5.   in vacuo   in a vacuum

II. Give the Latin word which means:

1.   womb   *utero*

2.   emptiness   *vacuo*

3.   place, position   *situ*

4.   a court case   *re*

5.   entirety   *toto*

III. Answer briefly. Sample answers are below:

1.   If archeologists are studying artifacts *in situ*, what are they doing?
     They are looking at the artifacts in the place they found them. They have not moved them.

2.   Why does the English word "vacuum" have two "u"s?
     The Latin word *vacuus* has two "u"s.

Exercises, p. 37

I.   Write the English meaning for each Latin expression:

1.   in vino veritas   in wine (there is) truth

2.   in vitro   in a glass container, in a test tube

3.   ipso facto   by the fact itself, by that very fact

4.   lapsus calami/lapsus pennae   slip of the pen

5.   lapsus linguae   slip of the tongue

II. Review the last ten expressions you have learned and then match:

1.   <u>D</u>   in vitro   A.   in the case (of)

2.   <u>J</u>   in utero   B.   in place

3.   <u>G</u>   ipso facto   C.   on the whole

4.   <u>F</u>   lapsus calami/lapsus pennae   D.   in a glass container

5.   <u>E</u>   lapsus linguae   E.   slip of the tongue

6.   <u>A</u>   in re   F.   slip of the pen

7.   <u>B</u>   in situ   G.   by that very fact

8.   <u>C</u>   in toto   H.   in wine (there is) truth

9.   <u>I</u>   in vacuo   I.   in emptiness

10. <u>H</u>   in vino veritas   J.   in the womb, unborn

Exercises, p. 39

I. Write the English meaning for each Latin expression:

  1. lapsus memoriae   slip of the memory

  2. libra (lb.)   weight, pound

  3. locum tenens   (one) holding a place, a substitute

  4. magna cum laude   with great praise

  5. magnum opus   great work, masterpiece

II. Fill in the blank with the Latin expression that is translated in the parentheses:

  1. The outstanding student will graduate _magna cum laude_ (**with great praise**).

  2. Many consider _Hamlet_ to be Shakespeare's _magnum opus_ (**masterpiece).**

  3. Have you ever suffered a _lapsus memoria_ (**slip of the memory**) when taking a quiz?

  4. The label on the bag of sugar said ten _lbs._ (**pounds**).

III. You should now know 95 Latin expressions commonly found in English. For the next week, look in magazines and newspapers, internet sites, and books. Find at least 3 of the phrases or their abbreviations and note them below:

Note to teachers: *e.g., i.e., etc., lb., in memoriam,* and *exit* are especially easy to find.

Answers will vary from student to student.

Exercises, p. 41

I.   Write the English meaning for each Latin expression:

    1.   mandamus   we command, order by a higher court

    2.   memento mori   be mindful of dying, remember (that you) are mortal

    3.   mea culpa   (by) my fault

    4.   mens sana in corpore sano   a sound mind in a sound body

    5.   mirabile dictu   amazing to say

II. Draw a scene with stick figures. Have one of the figures saying a Latin expression. A sample scene is below.

Exercises, p. 43

I.   Write the English meaning for each Latin expression:

   1.   modus operandi (M.O.)   way of operating

   2.   modus vivendi   way of living, lifestyle

   3.   morituri te salutamus   we (who are) about to die salute you

   4.   ne plus ultra   no more beyond, the pinnacle, the top

   5.   nemo est supra leges   no one is above the law

II. Supply the missing word:

   1.   morituri _te_ salutamus

   2.   _modus_ vivendi

   3.   ne _plus_ ultra

   4.   nemo est _supra_ leges

III. Give the meaning of these English words. Some sample answers are below.

   1.   vivacious = lively

   2.   exculpate = to clear of guilt

   3.   culpable = guilty

Exercises, p. 45

I. Write the English meaning for each Latin expression:

    1.   nihil per os   nothing by mouth

    2.   nil desperandum   nothing must be despaired of, never give up

    3.   nolo contendere   I do not want to contest, plea by a defendant essentially admitting guilt

    4.   non compos mentis   not sound of mind

    5.   non sequitur   it does not follow, an illogical statement

II. Abbreviations are always a little tricky. How many do you remember? Give the Latin and the English for each:

		Latin	English
1.	ibid.	*ibidem*	in the same place
2.	i.e.	*id est*	that is, in other words
3.	lb.	*libra*	pound
4.	M.O.	*modus operandi*	way of operating
5.	n.p.o.	*nihil per os*	nothing by mouth

Exercises, p. 47

I.   Write the English meaning for each Latin expression:

    1.   nota bene (N.B.)   note well, pay attention

    2.   novus ordo seclorum   new order of the ages, new world order

    3.   O tempora! O mores!   O the times! O the customs!

    4.   onus probandi   burden of proving, burden of proof

    5.   opus citatum, opere   work cited
            citato (op. cit.)

II.   Add the missing word to each expression:

    1.   novus ordo _seclorum_

    2.   O tempora! O _mores!_

    3.   onus _probandi_

    4.   opus _citatum_

    5.   nota _bene_

III.   Define. Some sample answers are below.

    1.   mores = morals, customs

    2.   approbation = approval

    3.   probation = period of time during which a person proves his worth

Exercises, p. 49

I. Write the English meaning for each Latin expression:

    1.   panem et circenses   bread and circuses

    2.   pater familias   father of the family

    3.   pax vobiscum   peace (be) with you

    4.   peccavi   I have sinned

    5.   per annum   by the year, annually

II. Fill in the blank with the Latin expression which is translated in the parentheses:

    1.   The family's income _per annum_ (**by the year**) was sufficient for their needs.

    2.   As we parted, my friend said, "_Pax vobiscum_ (**peace be with you**)."

    3.   To keep his people's favor the emperor promised _panem et circenses_ (**bread and circuses**).

    4.   The cruel _pater familias_ (**father of the family**) refused his daughter permission to marry.

III. Give meanings. Some sample answers are below.

    1.   impeccable = perfect

    2.   peccadillo = a little mistake

Exercises, p. 51

I. Write the English meaning for each Latin expression:

    1.   per capita   by heads, individually

    2.   per centum   out of each hundred

    3.   per diem   by the day, daily allowance

    4.   per se   by itself, intrinsically, directly

    5.   persona non grata   unwelcome person

II. Unscramble the second part of each expression:

    1.   per mied = diem

    2.   per muntec = centum

    3.   per pacita = capita

III. List as many English words as you can which are derived from *grata*. Some sample answers are below.

gratify
gratitude
gratuitous
grace
gracious
graceful
graceless
ungrateful
ingrate

Exercises, p. 53

I.   Write the English meaning for each Latin expression:

    1.   placebo   I will please, an inactive medicine given merely to satisfy a patient

    2.   pons asinorum   bridge of donkeys, Euclid's fifth proposition

    3.   post hoc, ergo propter hoc   after this, therefore on account of it

    4.   post meridiem (P.M.)   after noon

    5.   post mortem   after death, examination of a corpse

II. Write a short paragraph in which you use **three** of the expressions above. A sample answer is below.

    The police detective was immediately suspicious when he got a call at 11:30 **P.M.** from a school where the Geometry teacher had disappeared. Nothing was missing from the teacher's classroom. On the board, the proof of Euclid's fifth proposition was visible with the words **Pons Asinorum** clearly written in chalk. A lottery ticket for thousands of dollars lay on the teacher's desk. Had the math teacher won the lottery and simply left his job? "**Post hoc, ergo propter hoc**," said the principal when he heard the detective's report.

Exercises, p. 55

I.   Write the English meaning for each Latin expression:

    1.   post scriptum (PS)   written after, an afterthought added to a completed letter or book

    2.   prima facie   at first appearance, obvious on the face of it

    3.   pro bono publico   for the people's good, free

    4.   pro forma   on behalf of the form, for the sake of appearance

    5.   pro rata   according to a fixed share, in proportion

II.   Review phrases 126–135. Then complete the matching:

1.	I	pro bono publico	A.	at first appearance
2.	F	pro forma	B.	written after
3.	C	pro rata	C.	in proportion
4.	J	post hoc, ergo propter hoc	D.	after noon
5.	E	placebo	E.	fake medication
6.	H	pons asinorum	F.	for form's sake
7.	D	post meridiem (P.M.)	G.	after death
8.	G	post mortem	H.	Euclid's fifth proposition
9.	B	post scriptum (PS)	I.	free
10.	A	prima facie	J.	after this, therefore on account of it

Exercises, p. 57

I. Write the English meaning for each Latin expression:

    1.   pro se   on one's own behalf, in one's own defense

    2.   pro tempore   for the time being, temporarily

    3.   quis custodiet ipsos custodes?   who will guard the guards themselves?

    4.   qui tacet consentit   he/one who is silent consents

    5.   quidnunc   what now, busybody

II. It is time to look at abbreviations again. Write the Latin and the English for these abbreviations.

    1.   pro tem.   *pro tempore*   for the time being, temporarily

    2.   P.M.   *Post Meridiem*   after noon

    3.   PS   *post scriptum*   written after, an afterthought added to a completed letter or book

III. Describe a situation in which you might use the phrase *quis custodiet ipsos custodes*. A sample answer is below.

    A security firm is trying to interest a business owner in hiring his company to guard its warehouse. The business owner might question the security firm with the phrase, "Quis custodiet ipsos custodes?"

Exercises, p. 59

I. Write the English meaning for each Latin expression:

1. quid pro quo   something for something, tit for tat

2. quod erat demonstandum (Q.E.D)   that which was to be proved

3. quod vide (q.v.)   which see, refer to

4. rara avis   a rare bird, an unusual person

5. re   in the matter, thing, affair; regarding

II. Give an example of a situation in which someone might write *Q.E.D.* A sample answer is below.

On a math test when you have worked on a problem and you know you have the correct answer, you might write *Q.E.D.*

III. Give an example of a situation in which someone might offer *quid pro quo.* A sample answer is below.

When someone hits you, you hit him or her back.

Exercises, p. 61

I.   Write the English meaning for each Latin expression:

    1.   rebus   by things, a puzzle which uses pictures of things

    2.   recipe (Rx)   take, directions for cooking, symbol for a prescription

    3.   res ipsa loquitur   the thing speaks for itself, the situation is obvious

    4.   requiescat in pace   may he/she rest in peace
          (R.I.P.)

    5.   sanctum sanctorum   holy of holies, a very private place

II. Draw a *rebus*. Write out the English words you have represented visually. The sample rebus below stands for "I love you."

III. Do you have a *sanctum sanctorum*? Describe a real or imagined *sanctum sanctorum*. A sample answer is below.

    A small upstairs room far from the kitchen and family room where her family spent most of their time became the writer's *sanctum sanctorum*.

IV. Describe a situation in which someone might exclaim, "*Res ipsa loquitur!*" A sample answer is below.

    The girl looks at the high price of the dress and checks the small amount of money in her purse. Knowing that it is too expensive she says sadly, "*Res ipsa loquitur...*"

Exercises, p. 63

I. Write the English meaning for each Latin expression:

   1. S.P.Q.R.   The Senate and the People of Rome

   2. seriatim   in series

   3. sic   thus

   4. sic transit gloria mundi thus passes the glory of the world

   5. sine die   without a day, without a date set to reassemble

II. Give the Latin word from which each English word is derived. Then give the meaning of the English word.

   1. glorify   *gloria*   to honor with praise

   2. transit   *transit*   transportation

   3. mundane   *mundi*   secular, commonplace, ordinary

III. Make up an imaginary quotation from a famous person that would require you to use *sic*. A sample answer is below.

   "Give me library (sic) or give me death."
                                   – Patrick Henry

Exercises, p. 65

I.   Write the English meaning for each Latin expression:

1.   sine loco   without a place, without a place of publication listed

2.   sine qua non   without which not, the essential element, a necessity

3.   stare decisis   the decision stands

4.   statim (stat.)   immediately

5.   status quo ante   the condition in which things (were) before

II.   Answer briefly. Sample answers are below.

1.   Why would you write *s.l.* in a bibliography?
     You don't know where a book was published.

2.   If a peace treaty after a war says that the border between two countries will
     return to "*status quo ante*," what does it mean?
     The border will remain as it was before the war.

3.   What do doctors do when they hear "*stat*"?
     They hurry to the emergency.

4.   What is the *sine qua non* for you to get a good night's sleep?
     Clean sheets, comfortable bed, quiet room, etc.

Exercises, p. 67

I. Write the English meaning for each Latin expression:

    1.   stet   let it stand

    2.   sub poena   under penalty, a legal document summoning a person to court

    3.   sub rosa   under the rose, secretly

    4.   sui generis   of its own kind, unique

    5.   sui juris   in one's own right

II. Use one of the new expressions to answer each question:

    1.   What is a near synonym for a *rara avis*?
          sui generis

    2.   What Latin phrase could describe a secret mission?
          sub rosa

    3.   What expression would you find on a page in a corrected manuscript?
          stet

    4.   How can a lawyer ensure that a key witness will appear in court?
          sub poena

Exercises, p. 69

I.   Write the English meaning for each Latin expression:

    1.   summa cum laude   with highest praise

    2.   tabula rasa   blank slate

    3.   tempus fugit   time flies

    4.   terra firma   solid earth, firm ground

    5.   terra incognita   unknown land, undiscovered territory

II.   Complete each phrase with the missing Latin word:

    1.   tempus   *fugit*

    2.   tabula   *rasa*

    3.   terra   *firma*

    4.   terra   *incognita*

    5.   summa   *cum laude*

III.   Discuss John Locke's theory that the human mind is blank as a *tabula rasa* at birth. Do you think nature or nurture is more important in shaping a person's character? A sample answer is below.

    Before John Locke, most people believed that a person's character and intelligence were determined at birth by his genetic heritage. Locke, on the other hand, believed that character and intelligence were determined by experience and environment. It seems clear that both genetic heritage (nature) and environment (nurture) are important in human development.

Exercises, p. 71

I.   Write the English meaning for each Latin expression:

    1.   ultima Thule   farthest Thule, the farthest point, the limit of any journey

    2.   vade mecum   go with me, a reference book or handbook carried at all times

    3.   veni, vidi, vici   I came, I saw, I conquered, a piece of cake, a slam dunk

    4.   verbatim   word for word

    5.   verbum sapienti   a word to the wise (is) sufficient

II. Explain what is going on in this scenario. A sample answer is below.

The explorer ventured into *terra incognita*. She lost her precious atlas that had been her *vade mecum*. She crossed unknown mountains and seas, and as she seemed to approach *ultima Thule*, she longed for *terra firma*. At last, she reached her goal and cried, "*Veni, vidi, vici!*"

The explorer went into unknown land. She had lost her handbook and as she reached the limit of her journey, she wanted to be on solid ground. At last she arrived and crowed, "Slam dunk!"

Exercises, p. 73

I. Write the English meaning for each Latin expression:

1. versus (vs., v.)   against
2. vice versa   the order having been changed, turn and about
3. videlicet (viz.)   namely
4. vivat   may he/she live, long live...
5. viva voce   by the living voice, orally, aloud

II. Write out the English meaning of each abbreviation.

1. Q.E.D.   that which was to be proved
2. S.P.Q.R.   the Senate and the People of Rome
3. s.l.   without a place (of publication) listed
4. stat.   immediately
5. vs., v.   against

III. Unscramble and translate these words:

1. oevc = *voce* = voice
2. earsv = *versa* = changed
3. taviv = *vivat* = may he/she live, long live...
4. eivc = *vice* = the order

IV. Use the following phrases in English sentences that show their meanings. Sample answers are below.

1. vice versa
One group has lunch, the other studies, and then *vice versa*.

2. videlicet (viz.)
Our second president, *viz.* John Adams, was born in Massachusetts.

CHAPTER TWO

Answers to Chapter Two

Sententiae Latinae Review

Review Exercise: The Fabulous Forty, p. 76

Here is a list of forty important Latin words and phrases followed by exercises to help remind you what they mean. You can look up any you do not remember in the Sententiae section of your workbook.

		Literal translation:	More common meaning:
1.	ad hoc *3*	to this	for this purpose
2.	ad nauseam *7*	to sea sickness	to the point of disgust
3.	alibi *8*	elsewhere	defense of being elsewhere when a crime was committed
4.	alma mater *9*	nourishing mother	school or college attended, school song
5.	alumnus, alumna *10*	foster child	graduate of a school or college
6.	alter ego *11*	another self	perfect substitute or deputy
7.	bona fide *21*	in good faith	genuine
8.	carpe diem *23*	seize the day	enjoy today
9.	caveat emptor *26*	let the buyer beware	same as literal
10.	cornucopia *30*	horn of plenty	same as literal

Exercises 1–10, p. 77

I.   Fill in the blanks with one of the phrases 1–10:

1.   The accused burglar had a (an) _alibi_ (**defense of being elsewhere**) for the time in question.

2.   At Thanksgiving the table was decorated with a _cornucopia_ (**horn of plenty**).

3.   My mother reminded me _ad nauseam_ (**to the point of disgust**) to clean up my room.

4.   The discount is available only to _bona fide_ (**genuine**) students.

5.   My friend is an _alumna_ or _alumnus_ (**graduate**) of my old school.

6.   My friend and I have the same _alma mater_ (**old school**).

7.   The assistant secretary is the _alter ego_ (**deputy**) of the secretary.

8.   The principal appointed an _ad hoc_ (**for this purpose**) committee to look into the question of Saturday classes.

9.   A good motto for a bargain hunter is _caveat emptor_ (**buyer beware**).

10. "Seize the moment" could be a translation of the phrase _carpe diem_.

II. Match:

1.	F	horn of plenty	A.	carpe diem
2.	I	buyer beware	B.	alibi
3.	H	genuine	C.	ad hoc
4.	B	defense of being elsewhere	D.	alter ego
5.	A	seize the day	E.	alumnus
6.	G	old school	F.	cornucopia
7.	C	for this purpose	G.	alma mater
8.	D	deputy	H.	bona fide
9.	J	to the point of disgust	I.	caveat emptor
10.	E	graduate	J.	ad nauseam

Review Exercise: The Fabulous Forty (cont'd), p. 78

		Literal translation:	More common meaning:
11.	cum laude *35*	with praise, with honor	same as literal
12.	magna cum laude *94*	with great praise	same as literal
13.	summa cum laude *66*	with highest praise	same as literal
14.	dramatis personae *45*	the masks of a drama	(the cast of) characters in a play
15.	e pluribus unum *47*	out of many (ingredients) one (stew)	out of many (backgrounds, states) one (nation)
16.	emeritus, emerita *48*	with merit	retired
17.	ex libris *54*	from the books	from the library (of)
18.	ex officio *56*	from the office	by virtue of one's position
19.	ex tempore *58*	out of the time, at the moment	on the spur of the moment
20.	exit *61*	he/she leaves	way out

Exercises 11–20, p. 79

I.   Give the Latin phrase that you would most likely find in each setting:

    1.   a theater program: *dramatis personae*

    2.   a penny, a dollar bill, or the Great Seal of the United States: *e pluribus unum*

    3.   a bookplate: *ex libris*

    4.   the diploma of a very good student: *cum laude*

    5.   the diploma of an excellent student: *magna cum laude*

    6.   the diploma of a remarkably outstanding student: *summa cum laude*

    7.   the door out of an auditorium: *exit*

II.   Give the English meaning of each phrase from question I:

    1.   cast of characters, the masks of a drama

    2.   out of many (backgrounds/states) one (nation), out of many (ingredients) one (stew)

    3.   from the library (of), from the books

    4.   with praise, with honor

    5.   with great praise

    6.   with greatest praise

    7.   he / she leaves, way out

III.   Give the Latin word or phrase which means:

    1.   retired   emeritus, emerita

    2.   without rehearsal, on the spur of the moment   ex tempore

    3.   by virtue of one's office   ex officio

Review Exercise: The Fabulous Forty (cont'd), p. 80

		Literal translation:	More common meaning:
21.	habeas corpus *67*	may you have the body (of evidence)	right of citizens to avoid unlawful imprisonment
22.	homo sapiens *68*	wise human	human being
23.	in flagrante delicto *76*	in a burning crime	caught in the act, caught red-handed
24.	in absentia *74*	in one's absence	same as literal
25.	mea culpa *97*	by my fault	same as literal
26.	non compos mentis *109*	not sound of mind	same as literal
27.	non sequitur *110*	it does not follow	an illogical statement
28.	panem et circenses *116*	bread and circuses	same as literal
29.	pater familias *117*	father of the family	same as literal
30.	per capita *121*	by heads	individually

Exercises 21–30, p. 81

I.   Give the Latin phrase which means:

1.	in one's absence	*in absentia*
2.	my fault	*mea culpa*
3.	human being	*homo sapiens*
4.	not of sound mind	*non compos mentis*
5.	right of citizens to avoid unlawful imprisonment	*habeas corpus*
6.	caught in the act	*in flagrante delicto*
7.	an illogical statement	*non sequitur*
8.	father of the family	*pater familias*
9.	bread and circuses	*panem et circenses*
10.	individually	*per capita*

II.   Use five of the phrases in question I in English sentences to show that you know what they mean. Sample answers are below.

1.   The hero was honored *in absentia*.
2.   "*Mea culpa*," cried the waitress when she spilled the soup on her client.
3.   Linnaeus designated human beings as *homo sapiens*.
4.   A trust fund was established for the family member who was *non compos mentis*.
5.   *Habeas corpus* is an important legal tradition in the United States.
6.   The thief was arrested *in flagrante delicto*.
7.   Your essay presents a strong argument except for one *non sequitur* in the first paragraph.
8.   A Roman *pater familias* had the power of life and death over his household.
9.   The emperor promised *panem et circenses*.
10.   The *per capita* income in the city has risen in the last year

Review Exercise: The Fabulous Forty (cont'd), p. 82

			Literal translation:	More common meaning:
31.	per se	124	by itself	intrinsically, directly
32.	persona non grata	125	unwelcome person	same as literal
33.	pro bono publico	133	for the people's good	free
34.	quid pro quo	141	something for something	tit for tat
35.	sine die	155	without a day	without a day set to reassemble
36.	status quo ante	160	the condition in which things (were) before	same as literal
37.	sub poena	162	under penalty	a legal document summoning a person to court
38.	tabula rasa	167	blank slate	same as literal
39.	tempus fugit	168	time flies	same as literal
40.	terra firma	169	solid earth, firm ground	same as literal

Exercises 31–40, p. 83

I. Fill in the blanks with the Latin phrase which best completes the sentence:

1. After the rough sea I was glad to set foot again on *terra firma* (**firm ground**).

2. Locke believed that an infant's mind is a *tabula rasa* (**blank slate**).

3. The Senate adjourned *sine die* (**without a day set to reassemble**).

4. The sundial's legend read *tempus fugit* (**time flies**).

5. The attorney spent hours doing *pro bono* (**free**) work for clients who could not pay for his services.

6. The State Department declared the alien a *persona non grata* (**unwelcome person**).

7. The new agreement will maintain the *status quo ante* (**condition things were before**).

8. The poor condition of the road did not cause the accident *per se* (**by itself**).

9. If you return a kindness for a kindness, this is an example of *quid pro quo* (**tit for tat**).

10. The judge issued a *sub poena* (**a legal document summoning a person to court**) for the important witness.

II. Complete each Latin phrase with the missing word. Then translate the phrase:

1.	tabula	*rasa*	blank slate
2.	quid	*pro quo*	tit for tat
3.	terra	*firma*	solid earth, firm ground
4.	sine	*die*	without a day set to reassemble
5.	status	*quo ante*	condition things were before

Review Exercise: Verba Sapienti, p. 84

1.	L	quidnunc	A.		unknown land
2.	K	veni, vidi, vici	B.		word for word
3.	J	tabula rasa	C.		let it stand
4.	F	terra firma	D.		one of a kind
5.	O	sub poena	E.		time flies
6.	A	terra incognita	F.		firm ground
7.	M	vade mecum	G.		namely
8.	C	stet	H.		secretly
9.	H	sub rosa	I.		immediately
10.	G	videlicet (viz.)	J.		blank slate
11.	B	verbatim	K.		I came, I saw, I conquered
12.	N	status quo	L.		a gossip
13.	D	sui generis	M.		handbook
14.	E	tempus fugit	N.		situation as it stands
15.	I	statim (stat.)	O.		summons which threatens punishment for noncompliance

CHAPTER THREE

Answers to Chapter Three

Mottoes

Exercises, p. 87

I.   Sketch the Great Seal of the United States. (Hint: use a one-dollar bill):

II. Explain the similarity between the Latin phrase, *e pluribus unum*, and the English phrase, "a melting pot." A sample answer is below.

    The Latin phrase describes a soup or stew: a single dish made out of many ingredients. The phrase "melting pot" is used in English to describe the way American society is made up of people from lots of different cultures.

III. How does the phrase *e pluribus unum* also apply to the government of the United States? A sample answer is below.

    Although there are many (*pluribus*) states, the United States has one (*unum*) federal government.

Exercises, p. 89

I.   Write out **the Latin and the English** for the mottoes of Kansas, Oregon and Alabama:

1.   Kansas
ad astra per aspera
to the stars through difficulties

2.   Oregon
alis volat propriis
she flies by her own wings

3.   Alabama
audemus jura nostra defendere
we dare to defend our rights

II.   Answer these questions briefly:

1.   What is the motto of the Royal Air Force? How do you translate it?
per ardua ad astra = to the stars through difficulties

2.   What English word is related to the Latin word *jura*?
jury

III.   Complete the chart below:

	English derivative	Meaning of English derivative	Latin word	Translation of Latin
1.	asperity	sharpness, roughness	*aspera*	rough, difficult
2.	volatile	fickle, changeable, easily evaporated	*volat*	she flies
3.	alate	having wings	*alis*	by wings
4.	audacious	bold	*audemus*	we dare

Exercises, p. 91

I. Write out **the Latin and the English** for the mottoes of Wyoming, New Mexico, and Kentucky:

1. Wyoming
    cedant arma togae
    let arms yield to the toga, let war yield to peace

2. New Mexico
    crescit eundo
    it grows as it goes

3. Kentucky
    Deo gratias habeamus
    let us have thanks to God

II. Answer briefly:

1. What does the word *toga* symbolize in the motto *Cedant arma togae*? What does the word *arma* symbolize?
    toga = peace; *arma* = war

2. What did the Romans call people who wore trousers?
    bracati

III. Complete the chart below:

	English derivative	Meaning of English derivative	Latin word	Translation of Latin
1.	deity	god or goddess	*deo*	god
2.	gratify	please	*gratias*	thanks
3.	crescendo	a passage in music in which the volume grows louder	*crescit*	grows

Exercises, p. 93

I. Write out **the Latin and the English** of the mottoes of Maine, Arizona, and South Carolina. Be sure to give two mottoes for South Carolina:

1. Maine
    dirigo
    I direct

2. Arizona
    ditat Deus
    God enriches

3. South Carolina
    dum spiro spero
    as long as I breathe, I hope
    while there is life, there is hope
    animis opibus parati
    prepared in mind and resources

II. Answer briefly:

1. What does the ending *-o* on a Latin verb tell you to understand? (Hint: Look at the motto of Maine)
    the pronoun "I" is understood

2. To what tradition does the expression "As goes Maine, so goes the nation" refer?
    before computers, the early votes in Maine were used to predict the outcome of an election

3. Where does Arizona get its name?
    aridus = day + *zona* = belt, zone

III. Complete the chart below:

	English derivative	Meaning of English derivative	Latin word	Translation of Latin
1.	spiracle	breathing hole of an insect	*spiro*	I breathe
2.	inspire	influence, impel, arouse	*spiro*	I breathe
3.	dirigible	airship; able to be steered	*dirigo*	I direct

Exercises, p. 95

I.   Write out **the Latin and the English** of the mottoes of Massachusetts, North Carolina, Idaho, and New York:

  1.   Massachusetts
       ense petit placidam sub libertate quietem
       with a sword she seeks peaceful quiet with/under liberty

  2.   North Carolina
       esse quam videri
       to be rather than to seem

  3.   Idaho
       esto perpetuo
       be forever

  4.   New York
       excelsior
       higher

II. Answer briefly:

  1.   What is another word in Latin besides *ensis*, which means sword?
       gladius

  2.   Explain the derivation of the English word "appetite."
       Petit means "he/she seeks" in Latin, and when you have an appetite, you seek food.

III. Complete the chart below:

	English derivative	**Meaning of English derivative**	**Latin word**	**Translation of Latin**
1.	essence	the most important ingredient	*esse*	to be
2.	excel	to do better, surpass	*excelsior*	higher
3.	petition	request to a superior authority	*petit*	he/she seeks

Motto Review Exercises #1, pp. 96–97

I. Match:

1.	<u>C</u>	esse quam videri	A.	God enriches
2.	<u>D</u>	ad astra per aspera	B.	I direct
3.	<u>F</u>	esto perpetuo	C.	to be rather than to seem
4.	<u>H</u>	crescit eundo	D.	to the stars through difficulties
5.	<u>J</u>	alis volat propriis	E.	higher
6.	<u>I</u>	audemus jura nostra defendere	F.	be forever
7.	<u>E</u>	excelsior	G.	while there is life, there is hope
8.	<u>A</u>	ditat Deus	H.	it grows as it goes
9.	<u>G</u>	dum spiro spero	I.	we dare to defend our rights
10.	<u>B</u>	dirigo	J.	it flies on its own wings

II. Which is your favorite motto? Why?

Answers will vary from student to student.

III. Match the Latin word with its English meaning:

1.	<u>D</u>	ensis	A.	god	
2.	<u>A</u>	deus	B.	thanks	
3.	<u>E</u>	arma	C.	she seeks	
4.	<u>C</u>	petit	D.	sword	
5.	<u>B</u>	gratia	E.	weapons	

IV. List two mottoes that focus on each theme:

1. peace

   cedant arma togae (let arms yields to the toga, let war yield to peace)

   ense petit placidam sub libertate quietem (with a sword she seeks peaceful quiet with/under liberty)

2. religion/God

   annuit coeptis (He [God] has nodded at [our] undertakings, He [God] has favored our undertakings)

   Deo gratias habeamus (let us have thanks to God)

   ditat Deus (God enriches)

Exercises, p. 99

I. Write out **the Latin and the English** of the mottoes of Ohio, the District of Columbia, and Oklahoma:

    1.   Ohio
         imperium in imperio
         an empire in an empire

    2.   District of Columbia (D.C.)
         justitia omnibus
         justice for all

    3.   Oklahoma
         labor omnia vincit
         work conquers all

II. Answer briefly:

    1.   What is an English phrase that is very similar in meaning to *labor omnia vincit*?
         If at first you don't succeed, try, try again.

    2.   Can you translate a similar Latin phrase *amor omnia vincit?*
         Love conquers all.

III. Complete the chart below:

	English derivative	Meaning of English derivative	Latin word	Translation of Latin
1.	omnibus	anthology of all the works of a particular author	*omnibus*	for all
2.	invincible	unconquerable	*vincit*	conquers
3.	imperial	having supreme power	*imperium*	empire
4.	laborious	tedious	*labor*	work
5.	elaborate	elegant	*labor*	work

Exercises, p. 101

I. Write out **the Latin and the English** of the mottoes of West Virginia, Colorado, and Connecticut:

    1.   West Virginia
            montani semper liberi
            mountain people (are) always free

    2.   Colorado
            nil sine Numine
            nothing without God

    3.   Connecticut
            qui transtulit sustinet
            He (God) who transplanted sustains

II. Answer briefly:

    1.   Explain the word *transtulit* in the motto of Connecticut.
            The early colonists were "transplanted" from England.

    2.   Use the expression "willy-nilly" in an English sentence. A sample answer is below:
            You must pay your taxes willy-nilly.

III. Complete the chart below:

	English derivative	Meaning of English derivative	Latin word	Translation of Latin
1.	sempiternal	always, forever	*semper*	always
2.	numinous	supernatural	*Numine*	God
3.	sustain	maintain	*sustinet*	sustains

Exercises, p. 103

I. Write out **the Latin and the English** of the mottoes of Arkansas, Missouri, Maryland:

    1.   Arkansas
        regnat populus
        the people rule

    2.   Missouri
        salus populi suprema lex esto
        let the safety of the people be the supreme law

    3.   Maryland
        scuto bonae voluntatis tuae coronasti nos
        You (God) have crowned us with the shield of your goodwill

II. Answer briefly:

    1.   What do the letters S.P.Q.R. stand for? What does the phrase mean?
        Senatus Populusque Romanus = the Senate and People of Rome

    2.   What does the Latin word *scuto* mean?
        with the shield

III. Complete the chart below:

	English derivative	Meaning of English derivative	Latin word	Translation of Latin
1.	regalia	elegant attire	*regnat*	rules
2.	voluntary	willing	*voluntatis*	will
3.	salubrious	healthy	*salus*	health

Exercises, p. 105

I.   Write out **the Latin and the English** of the mottoes of Michigan, Virginia, and Mississippi:

1.   Michigan
        si quaeris peninsulam amoenam, circumspice
        if you seek a pleasant peninsula, look around

2.   Virginia
        sic semper tyrannis
        thus always to tyrants

3.   Mississippi
        virtute et armis
        by courage and arms

II.   Answer briefly. Sample answers are below.

1.   Why does the Michigan motto mention a peninsula?
        The state of Michigan is a peninsula.

2.   Explain the Latin derivation of peninsula.
        paene = almost + *insula* = island

3.   Describe the seal of Virginia.
        a woman with her foot on the neck of a tyrant

III.   Complete the chart below:

	English derivative	Meaning of English derivative	Latin word	Translation of Latin
1.	amenity	something pleasant, but not essential	*amoenus*	pleasant
2.	sic	thus	*sic*	thus
3.	armament	weapon	*arma*	weapons

Motto Review Exercise #2, pp. 106–107

I.   Match:

1.	D	imperium in imperio	A.	thus always to tyrants
2.	E	justitia omnibus	B.	by courage and arms
3.	F	regnat populus	C.	nothing without God
4.	C	nil sine Numine	D.	an empire in an empire
5.	I	labor vincit omnia	E.	justice to all
6.	B	virtute et armis	F.	the people rule
7.	J	montani semper liberi	G.	he who transplanted sustains
8.	G	qui transtulit sustinet	H.	let the safety of the people be the supreme law
9.	A	sic semper tyrannis	I.	work conquers all
10.	H	salus populi suprema lex esto	J.	mountain people (are) always free

II. Use **three** of these derivatives in sentences to show that you know their meanings: salubrious, amenity, numinous, invincible, regalia. Sample answers are below:

1.   New England has a **salubrious** climate.
2.   My favorite **amenity** in my new car is its heated seats.
3.   The poet was inspired by the **numinous** atmosphere of the forest.
4.   Our team is **invincible**.
5.   Everyone was decked out in full **regalia** for the ball.

III. Give one motto which focuses on each theme. Sample answers are below.

    1.   religion/God
        nil sine Numine (nothing without God)

    2.   freedom
        montani semper liberi (mountain people [are] always free)

    3.   justice
        justitia omnibus (justice to all)

    4.   law
        salus populi suprema lex esto (let the safety of the people be the supreme law)

    5.   a special characteristic of the state
        imperium in imperio (an empire in an empire)

IV. California's motto is the Greek word *Eureka*, which means "I have discovered (it)." What was discovered in California in 1848?

    gold

Exercises, p. 109

I.   Fill in the missing Latin word. Then translate the whole motto:

1.   certa _bonum_ certamen
     fight the good fight

2.   crescat _scientia_, _vita_ excolatur
     let knowledge grow, let life be perfected

3.   Dei sub numine _viget_
     under the providence of God it flourishes

4.   _eruditio_ et religio
     learning and religion

II.   Give the meaning and the Latin root for each of these English words:

English derivative	Meaning of English derivative	Latin word
1. vital	necessary to life	_vita_
2. vigorous	strong, active, robust, flourishing	_viget_
3. erudition	learning	_eruditio_

III. Answer briefly:

Does your school have a motto?
   A.   If it has a Latin motto, translate it. Find out who chose it and why.
   B.   If not, make up a motto and explain why you picked it.

Answers will vary.

Exercises, p. 111

I.   Fill in the missing Latin word. Then translate the whole motto:

1.   ex _scientia_ tridens
         from knowledge the trident, from knowledge power over the sea

2.   lux et _veritas_
         light and truth

3.   _lux_ fiat
         let there be light, let light be made

4.   ministrare quam _ministrari_
         to serve rather than to be served

II. Give the meaning and the Latin root for each of these English words:

English derivative	Meaning of English derivative	Latin word
1. veracious	truthful	_veritas_
2. translucent	allowing light to enter	_lux_
3. fiat	order, decree	_fiat_

III. Answer briefly:

1.   What does a trident look like? (You may draw one.) What Roman god had a trident as his symbol? Why is a trident an appropriate symbol for the US Naval Academy?
         A three pronged pitch fork = symbol of Neptune (Poseidon) who was the god of the sea.

2.   Why would a bumper sticker on the car belonging to a Lacrosse player from Yale read _LAX et Veritas_?
         LAX = lacrosse
         Lux = light
         It's a play on _lux et veritas_, the motto of Yale.

Exercises, p. 113

I.   Fill in the missing Latin word. Then translate the whole motto:

   1.   Numen *lumen*
        God (is) light

   2.   respice, adspice, *prospice*
        look to the past, look to the present, look to the future

   3.   terras *irradient*
        they will light up the lands

II.   Give the meaning and the Latin root for each of these English words:

English derivative	Meaning of English derivative	Latin word
1. luminous	bright, shining	*lumen*
2. conspicuous	obvious	*respice, adspice, prospice*
3. verity	established truth	*veritas*

III. Answer briefly:

   1.   What is the difference between *lux* and *lumen?*
        lux is daylight; *lumen* is lamplight

   2.   Why should students look to the present? the past? the future?
        Education means studying the past (history), the present (literature, languages), the future (science, technology).

Exercises, p. 115

I.   Fill in the missing Latin word. Then translate the whole motto:

1.   veritas vos *liberabit*
         the truth shall make you free

2.   *festina* lente
         make haste slowly

3.   vox *clamantis* in deserto
         a voice of (one) crying in the desert

4.   fortiter, feliciter, *fideliter*
         bravely, happily, faithfully

II.   Give the meaning and the Latin root for each of these English words:

English derivative	Meaning of English derivative	Latin word
1. acclamation	shout of approval	*clamantis*
2. felicity	happiness	*feliciter*
3. fortitude	bravery, courage	*fortiter*
4. fidelity	faithfulness	*fideliter*

III.   Answer briefly:

1.   Explain the paradox in *festina lente*.
         If you're hurrying, you're not slow, so the two words seem to contradict each other.

2.   Can you guess what Magnavox, a brand of audio equipment, means?
         Big Voice

Exercises, p. 116

I. Translate each Latin word:

1. curare   to care for

2. terram   earth

3. facta   deeds

4. verba   words

II. Which of the mottoes on this page is most appropriate for the organization it represents? Why? Sample answers are below.

> *curare*: caring is what a Medical Regiment does
> *descende ad terram*: parachuters must descend to earth
> *facta non verba*: deeds are more important than words for soldiers

III. True or False (Hint: Find the Latin root of the word in bold to help you with these statements.)

    False   1. If somebody is an **extraterrestrial,** he is from earth.

    False   2. A **verbose** individual says what he means in only a few words.

Exercises, p. 117

I.   Translate each Latin word:

1.   nunc   now

2.   numquam   never

3.   aut   or

4.   semper   always

5.   fidelis   faithful

II. Answer briefly:

1.   How is the word *fidelis* sometimes abbreviated? (Hint: Name a march by John Philip Sousa.)
     fi (Semper Fidelis, the Sousa march, is often called Semper Fi)

2.   What state motto includes the word *semper*?
     sic semper tyrannis (VA)
     montani semper liberi (WVA)

III. True or False (Hint: Find the Latin root of the word in bold to help you with these statements.)

____False____ 1.   "I am not interested in gossip," said the **quidnunc.**

____True____ 2.   A journalist who reports on an event with accuracy is said to have **fidelity** to the truth.

Exercises, p. 118

I.   Translate each Latin word:

    1.   arbor   tree

    2.   potestas   power

II.   Answer briefly:

    1.   Why do you think Lord Fairfax chose this motto? (Hint: say the Latin words aloud)
        The Latin sounds like Fairfax.

    2.   Explain the motto of the Atomic Energy Commission
        Atoms are very small, but when they're split, they create very great power.

III.   True or False (Hint: Find the Latin root of the word in bold to help you with these statements.)

    _____False_____   1.   In **horticulture** class students learn about bones and skeletons.

    _____True_____   2.   An **urban** dweller lives in a city.

Exercises, p. 120

I. Translate each Latin word:

1. leonem   lion

2. mentiri   lie

3. tangere   touch

II. Why do you think the Notley family chose their motto? (Hint: say the English translation aloud.)

   Notley sounds like "not lie."

III. Answer the questions based upon the meaning of the Latin root that is in bold type. Sample answers are below.

1. Name something that is **tang**ible: pen, book
2. Name something that could be described as **reg**al: a banquet

Exercises, p. 121

I.   Translate each Latin word:

    1.   ecclesia   church

    2.   mori   to die

    3.   vult   want

    4.   fiet   will be

    5.   sequor   I follow

    6.   sors   fate

    7.   fert...ferimus   bring...we bear

    8.   praeda   spoil

II. Which motto would you pick for your family? Why?

    Answers will vary from student to student.

III. Answer the questions based upon the meaning of the Latin root that is in bold. Sample answers are below:

    1.   Name something that should be **sequ**ential to something else:
           Latin II to Latin I

    2.   Name something that might need to be **rect**ified:
           a boundary dispute

CHAPTER FOUR

Answers to Chapter Four

Mottoes Review

Review Exercises: Mottoes, pp. 124–128

Here are the three mottoes of the **United States**. Translate all three mottoes.

e pluribus unum = one out of more, one out of many

annuit coeptis = He (God) has nodded at (our) undertakings, He (God) has favored our undertakings

novus ordo seclorum = new world order

Now, pick one of the three mottoes, and write two sentences telling why this phrase fits our country. Sample answers are below.

1. *E pluribus unum* meant a stew or soup, and it fits our country which is home to people of many different backgrounds. It also reminds us that we have many (*pluribus*) states and one (*unum*) federal government.

2. *Annuit coeptis* fits the United States because we have not finished building our nation. We are constantly embarking on new "undertakings."
    N.B. The word *coeptis* is related to the Latin verb *coepi* which means "begin," and the phrase on the dollar bill is on top of the unfinished pyramid, a symbol of our government as an unfinished project.

3. *Novus ordo seclorum* fits the United States because North America is part of the New World. Our democratic system of government was something new in world history.

What do these Latin words mean?

1. coeptis   undertakings

2. unum   one

3. novus   new

Here are twelve **state** mottoes. Translate each motto:

1.	ad astra per aspera	to the stars through difficulties
2.	alis volat propriis	she flies by her own wings
3.	animis opibusque parati	prepared in minds and resources
4.	dum spiro spero	while there is life, there is hope
5.	audemus jura nostra defendere	we dare to defend our rights
6.	cedant arma togae	let arms yield to the toga
7.	crescit eundo	it grows as it goes
8.	Deo gratias habeamus	let us have thanks to God
9.	dirigo	I direct
10.	ditat Deus	God enriches
11.	ense petit placidam sub libertate quietem	with a sword she seeks peaceful quiet with liberty
12.	esse quam videri	to be rather than to seem

Now, match the motto with its state:

1.	J	ad astra per aspera	A.	Massachusetts
2.	I	alis volat propriis	B.	North Carolina
3.	K	animis opibusque parati	C.	Maine
4.	K	dum spiro spero	D.	New Mexico
5.	F	audemus jura nostra defendere	E.	Kentucky
6.	G	cedant arma togae	F.	Alabama
7.	D	crescit eundo	G.	Wyoming
8.	E	Deo gratias habeamus	H.	Arizona
9.	C	dirigo	I.	Oregon
10.	H	ditat Deus	J.	Kansas
11.	A	ense petit placidam sub libertate quietem	K.	South Carolina
12.	B	esse quam videri		

Here are fourteen more **state** mottoes. Translate each:

1.	esto perpetuo	be forever
2.	excelsior	higher
3.	imperium in imperio	an empire in an empire
4.	justitia omnibus	justice for all
5.	labor omnia vincit	work conquers all
6.	montani semper liberi	mountain people (are) always free
7.	nil sine Numine	nothing without God
8.	qui transtulit sustinet	He (God) who transplanted sustains
9.	regnat populus	the people rule
10.	salus populi suprema lex esto	let the safety of the people be the supreme law
11.	scuto bonae voluntatis tuae coronasti nos	You (God) have crowned us with the shield of your good will
12.	si quaeris peninsulam amoenam, circumspice	if you seek a pleasant peninsula, look around
13.	sic semper tyrannis	thus always to tyrants
14.	virtute et armis	by courage and arms

Now, name the state whose motto fits the description below:

1.	speaks of tyrants:	Virginia
2.	mentions a peninsula:	Michigan
3.	has the word for shield:	Maryland
4.	refers to justice:	DC
5.	uses the word for empire twice:	Ohio
6.	uses a comparative adjective (ends in -er in English, -ior in Latin):	New York

Here are seventeen **college or school** mottoes. Translate the bold word in each:

1.	certa bonum **certamen** (Iona College, NY)	fight
2.	crescat **scientia**, vita excolatur (University of Chicago, IL)	knowledge
3.	**Dei** sub numine viget (Princeton University, NJ)	of God
4.	**eruditio** et religio (Duke University, NC)	learning
5.	ex scientia **tridens** (Naval Academy, MD)	trident
6.	**lux** et veritas (Yale University, CT)	light
7.	lux **fiat (**Albion College, MI; Alfred College, NY)	let...be made, let there be
8.	**ministrare** quam ministrari (Wellesley College, MA)	to serve
9.	numen **lumen** (University of Wisconsin, WI)	light
10.	respice, adspice, **prospice** (City College of New York, NY)	look to the future
11.	terras **irradient** (Amherst College, MA)	they will light up
12.	**veritas** (Harvard University, MA)	truth
13.	veritas vos **liberabit** (Johns Hopkins University, MD)	will make free
14.	**vox** clamantis in deserto (Dartmouth College, MA)	a voice
15.	**festina** lente (Madeira School, VA)	make haste
16.	aut **disce** aut discede (Winchester College, U.K.)	learn
17.	**fortiter, feliciter, fideliter** (Episcopal High School, VA)	bravely, happily, faithfully

Here are ten mottoes of **organizations or a family.** Translate each one:

1.	curare (11th Medical Regiment)	to care for
2.	descende ad terram (507th Parachute Regiment)	descend to earth
3.	nunc aut numquam (497th Field Artillery)	now or never
4.	semper fidelis (US Marine Corps)	always faithful
5.	semper paratus (US Coastguard)	always prepared
6.	arbor potestas (US Forestry Service)	tree power
7.	citius, altius, fortius (Olympics)	swifter, higher, stronger
8.	fare fac (Fairfax County, VA)	say (it), do (it)
9.	urbs in horto (Chicago)	a city in a garden
10.	noli mentiri (Notley)	don't lie

Now, give the Latin words for the following:

1.	city	urbs
2.	garden	horto
3.	tree	arbor
4.	always	semper
5.	now	nunc
6.	never	numquam
7.	power	potestas
8.	faithful	fidelis
9.	prepared	paratus
10.	faster	citius

CHAPTER FIVE

Answers to Chapter Five

Abbreviations

COMMON LATIN ABBREVIATIONS, p. 130

Fill in the chart below. This information was presented in chapter one of the Sententiae Latinae section of this book.

		Latin words	English translations
1.	A.M.	ante meridiem	before noon
2.	P.M.	post meridiem	after noon
3.	PS	post scriptum	after the writing
4.	etc.	et cetera	and the rest
5.	A.D.	anno Domini	in the year of the Lord, Common Era
6.	e.g.	exempli gratia	for example
7.	i.e.	id est	that is, in other words
8.	N.B.	nota bene	note well
9.	ad lib.	ad libitum	at pleasure, without rehearsal
10.	M.O.	modus operandi	way of operating
11.	pro tem.	pro tempore	temporarily
12.	vs., v.	versus	against
13.	C.V.	curriculum vitae	resume
14.	R.I.P.	requiescat in pace	may he/she rest in peace
15.	stat.	statim	immediately
16.	lb.	libra	weight, pound

Exercises: Common Latin Abbreviations, pp. 131–132

Fill in the blank with the abbreviation which best translates the phrase in parentheses:

1. Please check the label before you buy the flour: we need a ten _lb._ (**pound**) bag

2. When you apply for a position, you must submit a _C.V._ (**resume**).

3. The game today is Army _vs_. (**against**) Navy.

4. The detectives recognized the robber's _M.O._ (**way of operating**).

5. Before you take a test, you should organize your notes, make flashcards, _etc._ (**and the rest**).

6. The youngest children, _i.e._ (**that is**) the first grade, will be first in line.

7. Early aviators, _e.g._ (**for example**), Amelia Earhart, took great risks.

8. The speaker who lost his notes was forced to give his remarks _ad lib._ (**without rehearsal**).

9. The meeting will begin at 9:00 _A.M_ (**in the morning**) and should finish by 3:00 _P.M_. (**in the afternoon**).

10. On August 24, _A.D._ (**CE**) 79, Mt. Vesuvius erupted.

11. After signing the letter, I added a _PS_ (**after the writing**).

12. The notice on the bulletin board was headed _N.B._ (**note well**).

13. The Senate will elect a president _pro tem_. (**temporarily**) tonight.

14. The doctors hurried to the emergency room when they heard _stat_. (**immediately**).

15. The children decorating for Halloween made cardboard gravestones with _R.I.P._ (**rest in peace**) painted in large letters.

Give the Latin word or phrase and its abbreviation for each of the following:

1.	before noon	ante meridiem, A.M.
2.	after noon	post meridiem, P.M.
3.	after the writing	post scriptum, PS
4.	and the rest	et cetera, etc.
5.	in the year of the Lord	anno Domini, A.D.
6.	for example	exempli gratia, e.g.
7.	that is, in other words	id est, i.e.
8.	pound	libra, lb.
9.	immediately	statim, stat.
10.	rest in peace	requiescat in pace. R.I.P.
11.	resume	curriculum vitae, C.V.
12.	against	versus, v., vs.
13.	temporarily	pro tempore, pro tem.
14.	way of operating	modus operandi, M.O.
15.	without rehearsal	ad libitum, ad lib.
16.	note well	nota bene, N.B.

MORE LATIN ABBREVIATIONS, p. 133

Fill in the chart below:

		Latin words	**English translations**
1.	ca., c.	circa	around, approximately
2.	cf.	confer	compare
3.	et al.	et alia	and the others
4.	ibid.	ibidem	in the same place
5.	n.p.o.	nihil per os	nothing by mouth
6.	op. cit.	opus citatum, opere citato	work cited
7.	Q.E.D	quod erat demonstrandum	that which was to be proved
8.	q.v.	quod vide	which see, refer to
9.	Rx	recipe	take
10.	s.l.	sine loco	without a place of publication listed
11.	S.P.Q.R.	Senatus Populusque Romanus	the Senate and the People of Rome
12.	verb. sap.	verbum sapienti	a word to the wise
13.	viz.	videlicet	namely

Exercises for More Latin Abbreviations, p. 134

I. Match:

1.	J	The Senate and the People of Rome	A.	Q.E.D.
2.	I	work cited	B.	et al.
3.	A	that which had to be proved	C.	Rx
4.	B	and the others	D.	n.p.o
5.	C	take	E.	cf.
6.	D	nothing by mouth	F.	viz.
7.	F	namely	G.	s.l.
8.	E	compare	H.	verb. sap.
9.	G	without a place (of publication)	I.	op. cit.
10.	H	word to the wise	J.	S.P.Q.R.

II. Assume you are doing research for a report. Answer these questions briefly:

1. When can you use *ibid.* in a footnote?
    You use *ibid.* when you are citing exactly the same book or article immediately after your first citation. You can think of *ibid.* as ditto marks for an author and title.

2. When can you use *op.cit.* in a footnote?
    You are citing a source you used earlier.

3. What does *et al.* mean in the list of authors of a book you have consulted?
    There are several "other" authors in addition to those you have listed.

4. What does *viz.* mean in an article you have read?
    Namely.

5. What does *cf.* mean at the end of an encyclopedia article you took notes on?
    Compare.

CHAPTER SIX

Answers to Chapter Six

Abbreviation Review

Latin Abbreviations Review, p. 136

Fill in the chart below:

		Latin words	**English translations**
1.	ad lib.	*ad libitum*	at pleasure, without rehearsal
2.	A.D.	*anno Domini*	in the year of the Lord, Common Era
3.	A.M.	*ante meridiem*	before noon, in the morning
4.	ca., c.	*circa*	around, approximately
5.	cf.	*confer*	compare
6.	C.V.	*curriculum vitae*	resume, summary of a career, lap of life
7.	et al.	*et alia*	and the others
8.	etc.	*et cetera*	and the rest
9.	e.g.	*exempli gratia*	for example, for the sake of an example
10.	ibid.	*ibidem*	in the same place
11.	i.e.	*id est*	that is, in other words
12.	lb.	*libra*	pound, weight
13.	M.O.	*modus operandi*	way of operating
14.	N.B.	*nota bene*	note well, pay attention
15.	n.p.o.	*nihil per os*	nothing by mouth
16.	op. cit.	*opus citatum, opere citato*	work cited
17.	P.M.	*post meridiem*	after noon
18.	PS	*post scriptum*	after the writing, written after, an afterthought added to any completed letter or book
19.	pro tem.	*pro tempore*	temporarily, for the time-being
20.	Q.E.D.	*quod erat demonstrandum*	that which was to be proved
21.	q.v.	*quod vide*	which see, refer to
22.	R.I.P.	*requiescat in pace*	may he/she rest in peace
23.	Rx	*recipe, symbol for a prescription*	take, directions for cooking
24.	s.l.	*sine loco*	without a place of publication listed
25.	S.P.Q.R.	*Senatus Populusque Romanus*	The Senate and People of Rome
26.	stat.	*statim*	immediately
27.	vs.,v.	*versus*	against
28.	verb. sap.	*verbum sapienti*	a word to the wise
29.	viz.	*videlicet*	namely

Latin Abbreviations, p. 137

I.   Circle the abbreviation which correctly completes each sentence:

1.   The authors of the math textbook are listed as Webster, Williams, (et al.) / etc.

2.   The note on the patient's chart to prevent her from eating or drinking read (n.p.o.) / stat.

3.   The Senate elected a chairman ad lib. / (pro tem.)

4.   A great novel, i.e. / (e.g.,) *Pride and Prejudice,* often draws on the author's own experience.

5.   One book in my bibliography is listed q.v. / (s.l.)

6.   The new coach, (viz.) / cf. Mr. Brown, makes everyone run laps.

7.   The math student wrote S.P.Q.R. / (Q.E.D) beside each answer on the quiz.

8.   The job applicant was asked to submit a current M.O. / (C.V.)

9.   You should arrive at the airport at 6:00 (A.M.) / A.D.

10. The abbreviation (N.B.) / lb. highlighted the most important part of the new assignment.

II. Give the English meaning of each abbreviation you picked in exercise I:

1.   et al.   and the others

2.   n.p.o.   nothing by mouth

3.   pro tem.   temporarily, for the time-being

4.   e.g.   for example, for the sake of an example

5.   s.l.   without a place (of publication)

6.   viz.   namely

7.   Q.E.D.   that which was to be proved

8.   C.V.   resume, summary of a career, lap of life

9.   A.M.   in the morning, before noon

10. N.B.   note well, pay attention

III. Match each abbreviation with the place it is most likely to be found:

1.	<u>D</u>	bibliography	A.	Rx
2.	<u>F</u>	court case or sports event	B.	lb.
3.	<u>J</u>	date	C.	PS
4.	<u>A</u>	drugstore	D.	s.l.
5.	<u>C</u>	letter or e-mail	E.	R.I.P.
6.	<u>B</u>	a bag of sugar	F.	vs., v.
7.	<u>I</u>	invitation	G.	S.P.Q.R.
8.	<u>H</u>	patient's chart	H.	n.p.o.
9.	<u>E</u>	gravestone	I.	A.M.
10.	<u>G</u>	manhole cover or trashcan in Rome	J.	A.D.

IV. Write out the Latin words for each abbreviation in exercise III:

1. recipe

2. libra

3. post scriptum

4. sine loco

5. requiescat in pace

6. versus

7. Senatus Populusque Romanus

8. nihil per os

9. ante meridiem

10. anno Domini

Answers to Chapter Seven

Projects and Games with Additional Games and Activities

Answers to the Sententiae Certamen, pp. 140–142

1. cast of characters
   1. they all leave
   2. exit

2. He (God) has favored (our) undertakings
   1. new world order
   2. Vergil

3. *e pluribus unum*
   1. soup or stew
   2. out of many cultures (states) one nation

4. free
   1. additional information for the judge
   2. body of an offense, the basic element of a crime

5. graduated with a very high grade point average
   1. with great praise
   2. *vale* = good-bye or *dico* = to say

6. college or school attended, school song
   1. *alumna*
   2. *alumnae*

7. *anno Domini* = in the year of the Lord, Common Era
   1. around, approximately
   2. ca., c.

8. before the Civil War
   1. cause of war
   2. bombing of Pearl Harbor

9. *exempli gratia* = for example, for the sake of an example
   1. *id est* = that is, in other words
   2. *ante meridiem* = before noon, in the morning

10. *nota bene* = note well, pay attention
    1. *post scriptum* = written after
    2. *quod erat demonstrandum* = that which was to be proved

11. *modus operandi* = way of operating
    1. *modus vivendi*
    2. lively

12. the pinnacle, the top
    1. secretly
    2. unique, one of a kind

13. *mens sana in corpore sano*
    1. *rara avis*
    2. red-handed, in the act

14. let the buyer beware
    1. beware of the dog
    2. a store

15. in place of a parent
    1. a word to the wise
    2. one learns by teaching

16. seize the day, enjoy today
    1. (of) arms and the man I sing, I tell of wars and a hero
    2. Descartes

17. I came, I saw, I conquered
    1. You also, Brutus? Even you, Brutus?
    2. Augustus'

18. you were not present
    1. by virtue of one's office
    2. for this (purpose)

19. gladiators
    1. an English general
    2. Constantine

20. a slip of the tongue (*linguae*) and a slip of the memory (*memoriae*)
    1. *liber* = book, *libra* = weight, pound, balance
    2. from the books, from the library (of)

21. in a test tube
    1. into the midst of things
    2. in place, in its original position

22. nothing is made from nothing
    1. in a vacuum, in emptiness, without considering other factors
    2. in total, entirely

23. a date to reassemble has not been set
    1. temporary
    2. Cicero

24. a great work, a masterpiece
    1. a work of art may remain famous for generations, but human life is short
    2. art created for its own sake, not for money

25. to seasickness, to the point of disgust
    1. to the infinite, endlessly
    2. from the beginning

Additional Games

Docendo discitur means one learns by teaching, but some students learn best by playing a game. Here are four favorites that work well with sententiae, abbreviations, or mottoes:

1. Charades can be fun, and if the class works in teams, you can make a contest out of a review session of sententiae, abbreviations, or mottoes. It is a good idea to take a few minutes for students to plan the skits and to agree on the rules before they start to play.

2. Pictionary is another good way to help everyone learn a group of new phrases or mottoes.

3. Jeopardy takes planning, but pairs of students can write a group of questions in each category (e.g. state mottoes, common abbreviations, sententiae that have to do with legal expressions, etc.). One student in each pair should write the "answer" in large letters on notebook paper. A designated student can organize the questions and tape them in categories to the board in the classroom. Another student, or the teacher, can read the questions aloud to three volunteers while someone else keeps score. Do not forget to include daily doubles and final round questions.

4. Bingo can be another good way to review. After the class has covered twenty-five sententiae, abbreviations or mottoes, photocopy the blank bingo cards on the next page so that each student will have at least one card. Instruct the students to fill in the squares on the bingo card with the twenty-five Latin phrases in whatever order they choose. Keep a list of the English meanings. Cut the list of English meanings into small squares and put them in an envelope for the caller. Use bingo chips or small candies for markers. Play first for a straight line, then for full house.

Additional Activities

1. **Sententiae, abbreviation, or motto badges:**

   Each week have students make badges for themselves with a favorite *sententia,* motto, or abbreviation in Latin. Have them use bright markers and wear them around school. At the end of the week, put all the badges on a classroom bulletin board and use them for a quick, oral review. You may want to make a badge for yourself each day.

2. **Motto map:**

   If you have a large map of the United States on your classroom bulletin board, you can add labels with the Latin motto of each state as you present them each week in class. A student can type a key with the name of each state, its Latin motto, and the translation.

Grading Rubric for Poster Project, p. 143

Poster Project Grade

1. Latin phrase clearly written on front, translation on back   _____

2. Illustration fits the phrase   _____

3. Neat presentation   _____

4. Visually attractive   _____

5. Well chosen phrase   _____

Total:_____

Grading Rubric for the motto project p. 144

Motto Poster Grade

1. Choice of motto: _____

2. Translation of motto: _____

3. Accurate grammar: _____

4. Presentation:

     neat   _____

     attractive   _____

Total:_____

CHAPTER EIGHT

Sententiae Quizzes and Answers

Extra! Extra!

Students love extra credit. Each time you announce a sententiae quiz, you might want to include one or more of these phrases which do not appear in the workbook for extra credit.

1.	aetate (aet.)	aged
2.	arguendo	for the sake of argument
3.	a fortiori	for a still stronger reason
4.	a priori	valid independently of observation
5.	ad litem	for the particular legal action or proceeding
6.	ex parte	from or on one side only of a dispute
7.	locus classicus	classical source, a passage commonly quoted to illustrate or explain a subject or word
8.	loco citato (l.c.)	in the place cited
9.	terminus a quo	beginning, starting point
10.	terminus ad quem	a goal, a limiting point
11.	volens et potens	willing and able

Sententiae Quiz #1 (1–20), pp. 2–8

I. Match:

1. _____ ab ovo usque ad mala   A.   elsewhere

2. _____ alibi   B.   without preparation

3. _____ ad hoc   C.   from the beginning

4. _____ ad hominem   D.   for this purpose

5. _____ ad infinitum   E.   nourishing mother

6. _____ alumnus, alumna   F.   graduate of a school

7. _____ ad lib.   G.   endlessly

8. _____ alma mater   H.   personal

9. _____ ad nauseam   I.   to the point of disgust

10. _____ ab initio   J.   from beginning to end

II. Give the meaning of each Latin phrase:

1. ars gratia artis _____

2. arma virumque cano _____

3. ante meridiem (A.M.) _____

4. annuit coeptis _____

5. anno Domini (A.D.) _____

III. Look at the phrases in question II, and tell which one might be found in each situation:

1. a dollar bill _____

2. the opening screen of an MGM movie _____

3. on an invitation _____

4. the opening page of Vergil's *Aeneid* _____

5. in a history book _____

IV. Use these phrases in an English sentence to show their meaning:

1. alter ego _____

2. ars longa, vita brevis _____

3. ave atque vale _____

4. amicus curiae _____

5. ab ovo _____

Answers to Quiz #1

I. 1. J   6. F

    2. A   7. B

    3. D   8. E

    4. H   9. I

    5. G   10. C

II. 1. art for art's sake

     2. arms and the man I sing

     3. before noon, in the morning

     4. He (God) has favored (our) undertakings

     5. in the year of the Lord, common era

III. 1. annuit coeptis

     2. ars gratia artis

     3. A.M.

     4. arma virumque cano

     5. A.D.

IV. Sample sentences are listed below.

    1. Robin is Batman's *alter ego.*

    2. The artist, knowing that he was ill, always remembered the phrase *ars longa, vita brevis.*

    3. My friends came to the airport to say *ave atque vale* as I left on a trip.

    4. The lawyer submitted an *amicus curiae* brief to the judge.

    5. We will begin the review *ab ovo.*

Sententiae Quiz #2 (21–40), pp. 10–16

I.   Match:

1.   _____ cave canem   A.   compare

2.   _____ caveat emptor   B.   let the buyer beware

3.   _____ circa (ca., c.)   C.   beware of the dog

4.   _____ cogito ergo sum   D.   approximately

5.   _____ confer (cf.)   E.   a set of firm beliefs

6.   _____ corpus delicti   F.   with praise, honor

7.   _____ credo   G.   with a little disbelief

8.   _____ cui bono   H.   body of an offense

9.   _____ cum grano salis   I.   to whose advantage

10. _____ cum laude   J.   I think, therefore I am

II. Give the meaning of each Latin phrase:

1.   bona fide _____

2.   de facto _____

3.   de jure _____

4.   de minimis non curat lex _____

5.   de gustibus non est disputandum _____

III. Look at the phrases in question II, and tell which might apply in these situations:

    1.   your friend loves a kind of music you hate _____

    2.   someone is thinking about bringing suit for a broken pencil _____

    3.   you show your student identification card to prove that you should receive a discount in a store that gives discounts to genuine students _____

    4.   legal restrictions recorded on an old deed _____

    5.   housing patterns along ethnic lines, not enforced by law _____

IV. Use these phrases in English to show that you understand their meaning:

    1.   cornucopia _____

    2.   calvo turpius est nihil comato _____

    3.   curriculum vitae (C.V.) _____

    4.   carpe diem _____

    5.   casus belli _____

Answers to Quiz #2

I.   1.   C   6.   H

    2.   B   7.   E

    3.   D   8.   I

    4.   J   9.   G

    5.   A   10.   F

II.   1.   in good faith, genuine

    2.   in fact, from the fact, in reality

    3.   by law, from law

    4.   the law is not concerned with trifles, the law does not care about the smallest things

    5.   there is no accounting for tastes, concerning tastes there is no dispute

III.   1.   de gustibus non est disputandum

    2.   de minimis non curat lex

    3.   bona fide

    4.   de jure

    5.   de facto

IV.   Sample sentences are listed below.

    1.   The desk was a *cornucopia* of pens and pencils.

    2.   The bald man wore a hat because he knew *calvo turpius est nihil comato.*

    3.   You should update your *curriculum vitae* when you apply for a job.

    4.   Don't waste any more time! Do your homework now! *Carpe diem*!

    5.   The bombing was the *casus belli.*

Sententiae Quiz #3 (41–60), pp. 18–24

I. Match:

1.	____ de mortuis nil nisi bonum	A.	and the others
2.	____ de novo	B.	to err is human
3.	____ deus ex machina	C.	retired
4.	____ docendo discitur	D.	out of many (ingredients/ backgrounds) one (stew/ nation)
5.	____ dramatis personae	E.	anew
6.	____ emeritus, emerita	F.	about the dead (say) nothing but good
7.	____ errare humanum est	G.	god from the machine
8.	____ e pluribus unum	H.	one learns by teaching
9.	____ et alia (et al.)	I.	cast of characters
10.	____ dulce et decorum est pro patria mori	J.	it is sweet and fitting to die for one's country

II. Explain briefly what these two phrases meant to the Romans and what they mean today:

1. e pluribus unum _____

2. deus ex machina _____

III. Give the meaning of each Latin phrase:

1. ex cathedra _____

2. ex libris _____

3. et tu, Brute _____

4. ex officio _____

5. ex post facto _____

IV. Give the Latin and the English for each abbreviation:

1. etc. _____

2. e.g. _____

3. et al. _____

Answers to Quiz #3

I.   1. F   6. C

     2. E   7. B

     3. G   8. D

     4. H   9. A

     5. I   10. J

II. 1. Roman view = soup, stew

         American view = melting pot

     2. Roman view = actor flown on stage by a crane

         American view = artificial or impossible device used to end a play or novel

III. 1. with authority

     2. from the library (of)

     3. You also, Brutus? Even you, Brutus?

     4. by virtue of one's office

     5. retroactively

IV. 1. et cetera = and the rest

     2. exempli gratia = for example, for the sake of an example

     3. et al. = and the others

Sententiae Quiz #4 (61–80), pp. 26–32

I. Match:

1. _____ fiat lux   A. make haste slowly

2. _____ festina lente   B. let there be light

3. _____ exit   C. the end

4. _____ finis   D. they all leave

5. _____ exeunt omnes   E. way out

II. Complete the Latin for each phrase:

1. guardian spirit of the place = genius _____

2. human being = homo _____

3. foolish fire, mirage = ignis _____

4. caught red-handed = in flagrante _____

5. in place of a parent = in loco _____

6. in this sign you will conquer = in hoc signo _____

7. into the midst of things = in medias _____

8. ignorance of the law excuses no one = ignorantia legis neminem _____

9. may you have the body of evidence, the right to a speedy trial = habeas _____

10. in memory = in _____

III. Give the English for each phrase:

    1.   in re _____

    2.   in absentia _____

    3.   in extremis _____

    4.   ignoramus _____

IV. Give the Latin and the English for each abbreviation:

    1.   i.e. _____

    2.   ibid. _____

V. True or false:

    1.   _____ Schools stand *in loco parentis* to their students.

    2.   _____ The emperor Augustus had a vision with the words *in hoc signo vinces* emblazoned in the sky.

Answers to Quiz #4

I. 1. B

   2. A

   3. E

   4. C

   5. D

II. 1. loci

   2. sapiens

   3. fatuus

   4. delicto

   5. parentis

   6. vinces

   7. res

   8. excusat

   9. corpus

   10. memoriam

III. 1. in the matter (of)

   2. in one's absence

   3. at the point of death

   4. an extremely ignorant person

IV. 1. id est = that is, in other words

   2. ibidem = in the same place

V. 1. True

   2. False

Sententiae Quiz #5 (81–100), pp. 34–40

I. Match:

1. ____ in vitro   A. in the matter (of)

2. ____ in utero   B. in place

3. ____ ipso facto   C. entirely

4. ____ lapsus calami/lapsus pennae   D. in a glass container

5. ____ lapsus linguae   E. slip of the tongue

6. ____ in re   F. slip of the pen

7. ____ in situ   G. by that very fact

8. ____ in toto   H. in wine (there is) truth

9. ____ in vacuo   I. in emptiness

10. ____ in vino veritas   J. in the womb, unborn

II. Give the English:

1. lapsus memoriae _____

2. libra _____

3. locum tenens _____

4. magna cum laude _____

5. magnum opus _____

III. Fill in the blanks using these expressions, then translate the phrase:
mandamus, mea culpa, memento mori, mens sana in corpore sano, mirabile dictu

    1.   When she spilled coffee on her friend, the girl cried: _____

    2.   Our school motto is: _____

    3.   When Aeneas saw the monster, he exclaimed: _____

    4.   The gravestones serve as a: _____

    5.   The court issued a writ of: _____

Answers to Quiz #5

I. 1. D   6. A

    2. J   7. B

    3. G   8. C

    4. F   9. I

    5. E   10. H

II. 1. slip of the memory

    2. pound, weight

    3. substitute, holding a place

    4. with great praise

    5. a masterpiece, a great work

III. 1. mea culpa = my fault

     2. mens sana in corpore sano = a sound mind in a sound body

     3. mirabile dictu = amazing to say

     4. memento mori = remember you are mortal, be mindful of dying

     5. mandamus = we command, order of a higher court

Sententiae Quiz #6 (101–120), pp. 42–48

I. **Complete** each Latin phrase with the missing word, then **translate** the whole phrase:

1. panem et _____

2. pax _____

3. pater _____

4. nota _____

5. onus _____

6. opus _____

7. O tempora! O _____

8. nolo _____

9. non _____

10. non compos _____

11. morituri te _____

12. ne plus _____

13. nemo est supra _____

14. novus ordo _____

15. nil _____

II. Tell whether each statement is true or false:

1. _____ You might find the letters n.p.o. on the chart of a patient on a special diet.

2. _____ A good student probably has an efficient M.O. for studying.

3. _____ Your monthly salary is your pay *per annum*.

4. _____ *Peccavi* is translated "I have sinned."

5. _____ A millionaire may enjoy a luxurious *modus vivendi*.

III. Translate each phrase in question II:

1. n.p.o. = _____

2. M.O. = _____

3. per annum = _____

4. peccavi = _____

5. modus vivendi = _____

Answers to Quiz #6

I. 1. panem et circenses = bread and circuses

2. pax vobiscum = peace with you

3. pater familias = father of the family

4. nota bene = note well, pay attention

5. onus probandi = burden of proving, burden of proof

6. opus citatum = work cited

7. O tempora! O mores! = O the times! O the customs!

8. nolo contendere = I do not want to contend

9. non sequitur = it does not follow, illogical statement

10. non compos mentis = not of sound mind

11. morituri te salutamus = we who are about to die salute you

12. ne plus ultra = pinnacle, top, no more beyond

13. nemo est supra leges = no one is above the law

14. novus ordo seclorum = new world order, new order of the ages

15. nil desperandum = nothing must be despaired of, never give up

II. 1. false

2. true

3. false

4. true

5. true

III. 1. nothing by mouth

2. way of operating

3. by the year, annually

4. I have sinned

5. way of living, lifestyle

Sententiae Quiz #7 (121–140), pp. 50–56

I. Match:

1. _____ pro bono publico   A. at first appearance

2. _____ pro forma   B. written after

3. _____ pro rata   C. in proportion

4. _____ post hoc, ergo propter hoc D. after noon

5. _____ placebo   E. inactive medication given merely to
                                          satisfy the patient

6. _____ pons asinorum   F. for the sake of appearance

7. _____ post meridiem (P.M.)   G. after death examination

8. _____ post mortem   H. Euclid's fifth proposition in Geometry

9. _____ post scriptum (PS)   I. free

10. _____ prima facie   J. after this, therefore on account of it

II. Underline the best answer:

1. A daily allowance is a **per diem** / a **per annum.**

2. The student's high grades **per se** / **per centum** did make her a class leader.

3. The letter was merely a **pro forma** / **per capita** gesture.

4. The worried investor said, "**Qui tacet consentit.**" / "**Quis custodiet ipsos custodes**?"

5. I added a **PS** / **P.M.** to the e-mail.

III. Give meanings:

1. quidnunc _____

2. persona non grata _____

3. pro se _____

4. pro rata _____

5. pro tempore _____

Answers to Quiz #7

I. 1. I
    2. F
    3. C
    4. J
    5. E
    6. H
    7. D
    8. G
    9. B
    10. A

II. 1. per diem
    2. per se
    3. pro forma
    4. Quis ipsos custodies custodiet?
    5. PS

III. 1. busybody, gossip
     2. unwelcome person
     3. in one's own defense
     4. in proportion
     5. temporarily

Sententiae Quiz #8 (141–160), pp. 58–64

I. **Complete** the phrase with the correct Latin word. Then **translate** the whole phrase:

1. quid pro _____

2. rara _____

3. quod erat _____

4. res ipsa _____

5. resquiescat in _____

6. sanctum _____

7. sic transit gloria _____

8. sine qua _____

9. status quo _____

10. stare _____

II. Translate each Latin phrase:

1. statim (stat.) _____

2. seriatim _____

3. sic _____

4. Senatus Populusque Romanus _____

5. rebus _____

Answers to Quiz #8

I. 1. quid pro quo = tit for tat, something for something

2. rara avis = rare bird, unusual person

3. quod erat demonstrandum = that which was to be proved

4. res ipsa loquitur = the thing speaks for itself, the situation is obvious

5. requiescat in pace = may he/she rest in peace

6. sanctum sanctorum = holy of holies, a very private place

7. sic transit gloria mundi = thus passes the glory of the world

8. sine qua non = the essential element, without which not, a necessity

9. status quo ante = the condition as it was before

10. stare decisis = the decision stands

II. 1. immediately

2. in series

3. thus

4. the Senate and the People of Rome

5. puzzle with pictures of things, by things

Sententiae Quiz #9 (161–180), pp. 66–72

I. Give the **English** for these Latin words, then give **a Latin phrase** with the word:

1. rosa _____

2. tempus _____

3. terra _____

4. poena _____

5. tabula _____

II. Translate each Latin phrase:

1. stet _____

2. versus _____

3. sui generis _____

4. verbatim _____

5. summa cum laude _____

6. vade mecum _____

7. veni, vidi, vici _____

8. verbum sapienti _____

9. sui juris _____

10. viva voce _____

Answers to Quiz #9

I. 1. rose; sub rosa

    2. time; tempus fugit

    3. land; terra firma or terra incognita

    4. punishment; sub poena

    5. slate; tabula rasa

II. 1. let it stand

     2. against

     3. unique, of its own kind

     4. word for word

     5. with greatest praise

     6. go with me, handbook carried at all times

     7. I came, I saw, I conquered

     8. a word to the wise

     9. in one's own right, having full legal capacity

     10. aloud, orally, by the living voice

CHAPTER NINE

Motto
Quizzes and
Answers

Mottoes Quiz #1 (US through New York), pp. 86–94

I. Match:

1. _____ esse quam videri   A.   God enriches

2. _____ ad astra per aspera   B.   I direct

3. _____ esto perpetuo   C.   to be rather than to seem

4. _____ crescit eundo   D.   to the stars through difficulties

5. _____ alis volat propriis   E.   higher

6. _____ audemus jura nostra defendere   F.   be forever

7. _____ excelsior   G.   while there is life, there is hope

8. _____ ditat Deus   H.   it grows as it goes

9. _____ dum spiro spero   I.   we dare to defend our rights

10. _____ dirigo   J.   it flies on its own wings

II. Which state has a motto which mentions

1. stars _____

2. wings _____

3. God _____

4. rights _____

5. hope _____

III. Translate:

1. e pluribus unum (2 ways) _____

   _____

2. annuit coeptis _____

3. novus ordo seclorum _____

4. dirigo _____

5. esse quam videri _____

6. esto perpetuo _____

7. excelsior _____

8. dum spiro spero _____

9. crescit eundo _____

10. Deo gratias habeamus _____

Answers to Mottoes Quiz #1

I. 1. C

    2. D

    3. F

    4. H

    5. J

    6. I

    7. E

    8. A

    9. G

    10. B

II. 1. Kansas

    2. Oregon

    3. Arizona

    4. Alabama

    5. South Carolina

III. 1. out of many ingredients/cultures/states, one nation/stew

     2. He has favored our undertakings

     3. new world order

     4. I direct

     5. to be rather than to seem

     6. be forever

     7. higher

     8. as long as I breathe, I hope; where there is life, there is hope

     9. it grows by going, it grows as it goes

     10. let us have thanks to God

Mottoes Quiz #2 (Ohio through Mississippi), pp. 98–104

I. Match:

1. _____ imperium in imperio   A. thus always to tyrants

2. _____ justitia omnibus   B. by courage and arms

3. _____ regnat populus   C. nothing without God

4. _____ nil sine Numine   D. an empire in an empire

5. _____ labor vincit omnia   E. justice to all

6. _____ virtute et armis   F. the people rule

7. _____ montani semper liberi   G. He who transplanted sustains

8. _____ qui transtulit sustinet   H. let the safety of the people be the supreme law

9. _____ sic semper tyrannis   I. work conquers all

10. _____ salus populi suprema lex esto J. mountain people (are) always free

II. Pick one of the mottoes below. Tell which **state** the motto belongs to, then **translate** the motto:

si quaeris peninsulam amoenam, circumspice _____

_____

_____

scuto bonae voluntatis tuae coronasti nos _____

_____

_____

Answers to Mottoes Quiz #2

I. 1. D

    2. E

    3. F

    4. C

    5. I

    6. B

    7. J

    8. G

    9. A

    10. H

II. 1. Michigan

        if you seek a pleasant peninsula, look around

    2. Maryland

        You (God) have crowned us with the shield of Your good will

Mottoes Quiz #3 (Iona College through Chicago), pp. 108–118

I. Translate each Latin word:

1. veritas _____

2. vox _____

3. arbor _____

4. descende _____

II. Match:

1. _____ semper fidelis   A. deeds not words

2. _____ semper paratus   B. now or never

3. _____ aut disce aut discede C. make haste slowly

4. _____ nunc aut numquam   D. always faithful

5. _____ festina lente   E. always prepared

6. _____ facta non verba   F. either learn or leave

III. Translate:

1. curare _____

2. fortiter, feliciter, fideliter _____

3. vox clamantis in deserto _____

4. citius, altius, fortius _____

5. fare fac _____

6. urbs in horto _____

IV. Answer briefly:

Translate the motto of the Atomic Energy Commission, *de minimis maximum*. Then, explain why it is appropriate.

_____

_____

_____

Answers to Mottoes Quiz #3

I. 1. truth

    2. voice

    3. tree

    4. descend

II. 1. D

    2. E

    3. F

    4. B

    5. C

    6. A

III. 1. to care for

    2. bravely, happily, faithfully

    3. a voice of one crying in the wilderness

    4. swifter, higher, braver

    5. say (it), do (it)

    6. city in a garden

IV. A sample answer is below.

"From the smallest the greatest" is appropriate because an atomic bomb is made from splitting very tiny atoms and creates an enormous explosion

Mottoes Quiz #4 Family Mottoes, pp. 120–121

I.   Translate:

    1.   fortes fortuna iuvat _____

    2.   noli irritare leonem _____

    3.   noli mentiri _____

    4.   noli me tangere _____

    5.   non mihi, sed Deo et regi _____

    6.   non nobis, sed omnibus _____

    7.   non vi, sed mente _____

    8.   pro Deo et ecclesia _____

    9.   pro patria vivere et mori _____

II. **Complete** each motto, then **translate**:

    1.   quod sors fert _____

    2.   quae recta _____

    3.   quod Deus vult _____

    4.   pro lusu _____

III. Answer briefly:

Which motto belongs to the Notley family? Why is this motto appropriate for this family?

_____

_____

_____

Answers to Mottoes Quiz #4

I   1.   fortune helps the brave

    2.   do not irritate a lion

    3.   do not lie

    4.   do not touch me

    5.   not for me, but for God and king

    6.   not for us, but for all

    7.   not by force, but by mind

    8.   for God and church

    9.   to live and die for one's country

II.   1.   ferimus: what fate brings we bear

      2.   sequor: what (things) (are) right I follow

      3.   fiet: what God wants will be

      4.   et praeda: for sport and spoil

III.   A sample answer is below:

noli mentire = do not lie, and "not lie" sounds like Notley.

CHAPTER TEN

Abbreviations Quiz and Answers

Abbreviations Quiz

	Latin words	English translations
1. ad lib.		
2. A.D.		
3. A.M.		
4. ca., c.		
5. stat.		
6. C.V.		
7. et al.		
8. etc.		
9. e.g.		
10. ibid.		
11. i.e.		
12. lb.		
13. M.O.		
14. N.B.		
15. n.p.o.		
16. op.cit.		
17. P.M.		
18. PS		
19. pro tem.		
20. Q.E.D.		
21. viz.		
22. R.I.P.		
23. Rx		
24. s.l.		
25. S.P.Q.R.		

Answers to Abbreviations Quiz

		Latin words	**English translations**
1.	ad lib.	*ad libitum*	at pleasure, without rehearsal
2.	A.D.	*anno Domini*	In the Year of the Lord, Common Era
3.	A.M.	*ante meridiem*	before noon
4.	ca., c.	*circa*	around, approximately
5.	stat.	*statim*	immediately
6.	C.V.	*curriculum vitae*	resume, summary of a career, lap of life
7.	et al.	*et alia*	and the others
8.	etc.	*et cetera*	and the rest
9.	e.g.	*exempli gratia*	for example
10.	ibid.	*ibidem*	in the same place
11.	i.e.	*id est*	that is, in other words
12.	lb.	*libra*	pound
13.	M.O.	*modus operandi*	way of operating
14.	N.B.	*nota bene*	note well
15.	n.p.o.	*nihil per os*	nothing by mouth
16.	op.cit.	*opus citatum, opere citato*	work cited
17.	P.M.	*post meridiem*	after noon
18.	PS	*post scriptum*	after the writing
19.	pro tem.	*pro tempore*	temporarily
20.	Q.E.D.	*quod erat demonstrandum*	that which was to be proved
21.	viz.	*videlicet*	namely
22.	R.I.P.	*requiescat in pace*	may he/she rest in peace
23.	Rx	*recipe*	take
24.	s.l.	*sine loco*	without a place of publication listed
25.	S.P.Q.R.	*Senatus Populusque Romanus*	The Senate and People of Rome

CHAPTER ELEVEN:

Oral Questions and Answers for Latin Students

Sententiae 1–20 Questions for Latin Students

N.B. These questions are designed to be asked orally of students who are taking a Latin language course. You might begin by asking students to look at the sententiae as they are listed in Appendix #1. Make sure that they remember how to translate each expression. Have students keep the list out so they can see the Latin word or phrase when you ask the grammar question(s). Some of the questions cover topics like deponent verbs, gerunds, and hortatory subjunctive which are usually covered in Latin II. You will probably want to skip these questions with younger students although it can be helpful for students to recall these examples later when they do encounter these grammatical constructions.

1. What case is *ovo* in the expression *ab ovo?* What determines the case here?
   * ablative
   * the preposition *a, ab* takes the ablative

2. What gender is *ovum?* How do you know?
   * neuter
   * *ovum* ends with the letters -um

3. Decline *ovum:*
   * ovum, ovi, ovo, ovum, ovo
   * ova, ovorum, ovis,ova, ovis
     N.B. The word for sheep in Latin is *ovis!*

4. Find three other neuter nouns in the first twenty sententiae:
   * infinitum, initium, libitum, bellum

5. What case is *hominem* in the expression *ad hominem?* What determines the case here?
   * accusative
   * the preposition *ad* takes the accusative

6. Find two other sententiae which have the preposition *ad* plus an accusative noun:
   * ad infinitum
   * ad libitum
   * ad nauseam

7. What case does the preposition *ante* take? Find an example in the first twenty sententiae:
   * accusative
   * ante meridiem
   * ante bellum

8. What gender is *alumna?* What declension is it? Decline *alumna:*
   - feminine
   - first declension
   - alumna, alumnae, alumnae, alumnam, alumna
     alumnae, alumnarum, alumnis, alumnas, alumnis

9. What case is *curiae* in *amicus curiae* and *artis* in *ars gratia artis?* What English preposition do you use to translate each of these Latin words?
   - genitive
   - "of"

10. Which of the first twenty sententiae has two singular imperatives:
   - ave atque vale

Sententiae 21–40 Questions for Latin Students

1. Why is *bona* ablative singular feminine in the expression *bona fide?*
   - *bona* agrees in gender, number, and case with *fide* which is ablative singular feminine; N.B. a good way to remember that adjectives in Latin have the same gender, number, and case as the nouns they modify is to say the rhyme "adjectives agree in g, n, c [gender, number, case]!"

2. Find two regular singular imperatives:
   - carpe (in *carpe diem*)
   - cave (in *cave canem*)

3. What case is *grano* in *cum grano salis* and *laude* in *cum laude?* Why?
   - ablative
   - because the preposition *cum* takes the ablative

4. What case is *facto* in *de facto, gustibus* in *de gustibus non est disputandum, jure* in *de jure,* and *minimis* in *de minimis non curat lex?* Why?
   - ablative
   - because the preposition *de* takes the ablative

5. What case is *cui* in cui bono? What pronoun does *cui* come from?
   - dative
   - the relative pronoun *qui, quae, quod*

6. Find a noun in the genitive from the sententiae #21–40. Translate each:
   - belli = **of** war
   - delicti = **of** the crime
   - salis = **of** salt
   - vitae = **of** life

7. Which word is the subject of *curat* in *de minimis non curat lex?*
    *   lex

8. What pronoun is implied in the verbs *credo, cogito,* and *sum?*
    *   "I"

9. What case is *canem* in *cave canem* and *diem* in *carpe diem?*
    *   accusative of direct object

10. What adjective in the superlative gives us *minimis* in *de minimis non curat lex?*
    *   parvus [comparative = *minor*; superlative = *minimus*]

Sententiae 41–60 Questions for Latin Students

1. What does the Latin preposition *ex* mean? What case does it take? Give an example from sententiae #41–60 that includes *ex.*
    *   from, out of
    *   ablative
    *   ex cathedra, ex libris, ex nihilo nihil fit; ex officio, ex post facto, ex tempore

2. What is another form of the preposition *ex?* When is this form used? Give an example of a phrase that uses the alternative form of *ex.*
    *   e
    *   the object of the preposition begins with a consonant
    *   e pluribus unum

3. What gender and number is *emeritus?*
    *   masculine, singular

4. What gender and number is *emerita?*
    *   feminine, singular

5. What case and number is *dramatis* in *dramatis personae?*
    *   genitive, singular (*dramatis* = of a drama)

6. In the expression, *de mortuis nil nisi bonum, nil* means "nothing." What is another way to write "nothing" in Latin? Give an expression with the longer form:
    *   nihil
    *   ex nihilo nihil fit

7. What form of the verb is *errare* in *errare humanum est?*
    *   present active infinitive used as a subject

8. What form of the verb is *mori* in *dulce et decorum est pro patria mori?*
    *   present deponent infinitive

9. Why does *Brute* end in the letter -e in the expression *et tu Brute?*
    *   *Brute* is vocative singular of a second declension masculine noun ending in -us

10. What do we call a verbal noun like *docendo* in *docendo discitur?* How is it translated?
    *   gerund
    *   by learning

Sententiae 61–80 Questions for Latin Students

1. Here are several Latin verbs from sententiae #61–80: *habeas* (from *habeas corpus*), *exit*, *ignoramus*, *exeunt* (from *exeunt omnes*). Give the pronoun subject that is understood for each ending:
    *   -s = you (singular)
    *   -t = he/she/it
    *   -mus = we
    *   -nt = they

2. What form of the Latin verb *festino* is *festina* in the expression *festina lente?* What part of speech is *lente?*
    *   imperative singular
    *   adverb

3. What is the genitive of the phrase *homo sapiens?*
    *   hominis sapientis

4. What verb gives us *est* in the expression *id est?* Give the principal parts and present tense. What pronoun has *id* as its nominative singular neuter?
    *   *sum, esse, fui, futurus* = to be
    *   sum, es, est, sumus, estis, sunt
    *   is, ea id

5. What case does the Latin preposition *in* take when it means "in" or "on"? Give an example from sententiae #61–80:
    *   ablative
    *   in absentia, in extremis, in flagrante delicto, in hoc signo, in loco

6. What case are *res* in the expression *in medias res* and *memoriam* in the expression *in memoriam?*
    *   accusative

7. The expression *in memoriam* means "in memory," but, more often in Latin, the preposition *in* with the accusative has a different meaning. What does *in* with the accusative usually mean?
    * into, against

8. What person is *vinces* from *in hoc signo vinces?* What tense is *vinces?* How can you tell? Give the principal parts of *vinco.*
    * second person singular (you)
    * future
    * -e is the tense sign of the future tense for third conjugation verbs (except for first person singular which has -a as the tense sign). Think of the mnemonic "future one and two -bo, -bi, -bu; future three and four, -a and -e forever more.
    * *vinco, -ere, vici, victum* = conquer

9. What is the nominative of *neminem* from *ignorantia legis neminem excusat?*
    * nemo

10. What is the nominative of *legis* from *ignorantia legis neminem excusat?*
    * lex

Sententiae 81–100 Questions for Latin Students

1. What declension is the Latin word *re,* found in the expression *in re?* Decline *res:*
    * fifth
    * res, rei, rei, rem, re
      res, rerum, rebus, res, rebus

2. What declension is the Latin word *situ,* found in the expression *in situ?* Decline *situs:*
    * fourth
    * situs, situs, situi, situm,situ
      situs, situum, sitibus, situs, sitibus

3. What declension is the Latin word *veritas,* found in the expression *in vino veritas?* Decline *veritas:*
    * third
    * veritas, veritatis, veritati, veritatem, veritate
      veritates, veritatum, veritatibus, veritates, veritatibus

4. What declension is the Latin word *calami,* found in the expression *lapsus calami?* Decline *calamus:*
    * second
    * calamus, calami, calamo, calamum, calamo
      calami, calamorum, calamis, calamos, calamis

5. What declension is the Latin word *linguae* found in the expression *lapsus linguae?* Decline *lingua*:
   * first
   * lingua, linguae, linguae, linguam, lingua
     linguae, linguarum, linguis, linguas, linguis

6. What case does the Latin preposition *in* take when it means "in" or "on"? Give an example from sententiae # 81–100:
   * ablative
   * in re, in situ, in toto, in utero, in vacuo, in vino, in vitro

7. What case are the Latin words *magna* and *laude* in the expression *magna cum laude?* Why?
   * ablative
   * *cum* takes the ablative, this expressions answers the question "how" and is an ablative of manner

8. What is the gender of the Latin word *opus* in the expression *magnum opus?* Decline the phrase:
   * neuter
   * magnum opus, magni operis, magno operi, magnum opus, magno opere
     magna opera, magnorum operum, magnis operibus, magna opera, magnis operibus

9. What is the tense, voice, person, and number of *mandamus?*
   * present, active, first person plural

10. What do we call a verbal adjective like *tenens* in the phrase *locum tenens?* What verb does *tenens* come from? How is it translated?
    * present participle
    * *teneo, tenere, tenui, tentum* = hold
    * holding

Sententiae 101–120 Questions for Latin Students

1. What do we call a verbal noun like *vivendi* in the expression *modus vivendi?* Find another example in sententiae #102–120:
   * gerund
   * onus probandi

2. What kind of participle is *morituri* in the expression *morituri te salutamus?* How is it translated?
   * future active
   * about to die

3. What case is *os* in the expression *nihil per os?* What determines its case?
    *   accusative
    *   the preposition *per* takes the accusative

4. What case does the Latin preposition *supra* take? Find an example in sententiae #102–120:
    *   accusative
    *   nemo est supra leges

5. In the expression *pax vobiscum,* where is the Latin preposition translated "with"?
    *   *cum* follows its object *vobis*

6. What form of the verb is *contendere* in the expression *nolo contendere?*
    *   present active infinitive used as an object

7. What case is *seclorum* in the expression *novus ordo seclorum?* How is the nominative singular usually spelled?
    *   genitive plural
    *   saeculum

8. What is the case of *familias* in the expression *pater familias?*
    *   archaic genitive (of the family) instead of the more familiar –ae

9. What is the nominative of *mentis* in the expression *non compos mentis?*
    *   mens

10. What form of the verb is *peccavi?*
    *   first person singular perfect active of the verb *pecco, peccare, peccavi, peccatum* = sin

Sententiae 121–140 Questions for Latin Students

1. List three Latin prepositions from sententiae #121–140 that take the accusative:
    *   per, propter, and post

2. Find a Latin preposition from sententiae #121–140 that takes the ablative:
    *   pro

3. What kind of pronoun is *se* in the expressions *per se* and *pro se?* In a Latin
    sentence how do you determine the meaning of *se?* Decline *se:*
    - reflexive
    - a reflexive pronoun takes its meaning from the subject of the sentence
      e.g. *Narcissus **se** videt.* = Narcissus sees **himself**.
      *Juno **sibi** multa dicit.* = Juno says many things to **herself**.
      *Custodes pecuniam **sibi** servant.* = The guards keep the money for
      themselves.
    - sui, sibi, se, se

4. In the expression *quis custodiet custodes ipsos,* how do you translate *ipsos?* How is
    ipse, ipsa, ipsum different from *sui, sibi, se, se?*
    - themselves
    - *ipse* is an adjective used for emphasis, *se* is a pronoun which is an integral
      part of the sentence. If you can omit the "self" word, and still have a
      sensible, complete thought, the Latin will have a form of *ipse*.

5. What tense is *custodiet* in the expression *quis custodiet custodes ipsos?*
    - future

6. What tense is *placebo?*
    - future

7. Find an example of an interrogative pronoun from sententiae #121–140:
    - **quis** custodiet custodes ipsos?
    - or **quid**nunc

8. Decline the interrogative pronoun singular and plural:
    - quis quid
      cuius cuius
      cui cui
      quem quid
      quo quo

    - qui quae quae
      quorum quarum quorum
      quibus quibus quibus
      quos quas quae
      quibus quibus quibus

9. Find an example of a relative pronoun from sententiae #121–140:
    - *qui tacet consentit*

10. Decline the relative pronoun singular and plural:
    - qui quae quod
      cuius cuius cuius
      cui cui cui
      quem quam quod
      quo qua quo

    - qui quae quae
      quorum quarum quorum
      quibus quibus quibus
      quos quas quae
      quibus quibus quibus

Sententiae 141–160 Questions for Latin Students

1. What case follows the Latin preposition *pro*, i.e. what case is *quo* in the expression *quid pro quo?*
   - ablative

2. What do we call a verbal adjective like *demonstrandum* in the expression *quod erat demonstandum?*
   - gerundive

3. What form of the verb are *vide* in *quod vide* and *recipe?*
   - imperative singular

4. What is the gender of *avis* in the expression *rara avis?* How can you tell?
   - feminine
   - *rara*, which agrees in gender, number, and case, modifies *avis*

5. Some Latin adverbs like *lente* end in the letter -e, but others end in -tim. Find two adverbs from sententiae #141–160 that end in -tim:
   - *seriatim* and *verbatim*

6. What kind of verb is *loquitur* in the expression *res ipsa loquitur?*
   - deponent, i.e. a verb with passive endings, translated actively

7. What noun do both *re* and *rebus* come from? What case is each?
   - res
   - ablative (*re* = ablative singular; *rebus* = ablative plural)

8. What is the subject of the verb *transit* in the expression *sic transit gloria mundi?*
   - gloria

9.   What form of the verb is *stare* in the expression *stare decisis?*
   - present, active infinitive of *sto, stare, steti, statum*

10.   What case does the Latin preposition *sine* take? List three examples from sententiae #141–160:
   - ablative
   - sine die, sine loco, sine qua non

Sententiae 161–180 Questions for Latin Students

1.   What is the tense and mood of *stet?* How do you recognize this tense and mood?
   - present subjunctive
   - first conjugation verbs like *sto, stare, steti, statum* have the key vowel -e in present subjunctive. Think of the mnemonic "Let's eat caviar" when you need to remember the key vowels of present subjunctive.

2.   What kind of subjunctive does *stet* illustrate?
   - hortatory, i.e. a polite command translated with "let"

3.   What case does the Latin preposition *sub* usually take? List two examples from sententiae #161–180:
   - ablative
   - sub poena, sub rosa

4.   What Latin possessive adjective gives us *sui* in the expressions *sui generis* and *sui juris?*
   - *suus, -a, -um* = his own, her own, its own, their own

5.   What is the nominative of the *generis?* What is its gender? Give its declension singular and plural:
   - genus
   - neuter
   - genus, generis, generi, genus, genere
     genera, generum, generibus, genera, generibus

6.   What Latin word is translated "with" in the expression *vade mecum?*
   - me**cum**: the preposition and its object are reversed just as they were in the expression *pax vobis**cum**.*

7.   Give the principal parts and meanings of each verb in the phrase *veni, vidi, vici:*
   - *venio, venire, veni, ventum* = come
   - *video, videre, vidi, visum* = see
   - *vinco, vincere, vici, victum* = conquer

8. What case are *sapienti* or *sapientibus* in the expression *verbum (sat) sapienti (sapientibus)*? What English preposition is implied with this case?
    *   dative
    *   "to"/"for"

9. What construction do we see in the expression *vice versa*? N.B. There are two words in the ablative, one is a noun and the other is a past participle.
    *   ablative absolute

10. What case is *voce* in the expression *viva voce*? Decline the word singular and plural:
    *   ablative
    *   vox, vocis, voci, vocem, voce
        voces, vocum, vocibus, voces, vocibus

Motto Questions for Latin Students, p. 86

N.B. These questions, like those for the sententiae, are intended to be part of oral class work. It may be helpful to have students write the mottoes from each page on the board so that everyone can see them as you ask the grammar questions.

1. What is another way to write the preposition *e*?
    * ex

2. What case does *e* take, i.e. what case is *pluribus*?
    * ablative

3. What gender is *unum*?
    * neuter

4. What pronoun subject do we supply for a verb like *annuit* that ends in -t?
    * he/she/it

5. What case is *seclorum*?
    * genitive plural

p. 88

1. What case does *ad* take?
    * accusative

2. Why do we add "by" or "by means of" when we translate *alis...propriis*?
    * ablative of means

3. What case, number, and gender are *astra*, *aspera*, and *jura*?
    * accusative plural neuter

4. What verb does *audemus* come from?
    * *audeo* = to dare (not *audio* = to hear)

5. What grammatical form is *defendere*?
    * second principal part = present active infinitive

p. 90

1.   What case is *togae?*
     *   dative

2.   What English preposition do we add to the dative when we translate?
     *   "to"/"for"

3.   What Latin verb means "go"?
     *   eo, ire, ivi, itum

4.   What case is *Deo?*
     *   dative

5.   How is *habeamus* translated?
     *   "let us have" because *habeamus* is hortatory subjunctive, a polite imperative

p. 92

1.   Find three Latin first person verbs on this page.
     *   dirigo, spiro, spero

2.   What case is *Deus?*
     *   nominative

3.   What third person singular verb is on this page?
     *   ditat

p. 94

1.   What case is *ense?*
     *   ablative

2.   What case is *libertate?*
     *   ablative

3.   What grammatical form of *sum* is *esse?*
     *   infinitive

4.   What form of *sum* is *esto?*
     *   imperative singular

5.   What does the ending -ior tell us about *excelsior?*
     *   -ior is comparative

p. 98

1. What gender is *imperium*?
    * neuter

2. How can you tell the gender of *imperium*?
    * the -um ending

3. What case is *omnibus*?
    * dative plural

4. What case is *omnia*?
    * accusative plural

5. What tense is *vincit*?
    * present

p. 100

1. What does the Latin adjective *liber, libera, liberum* mean?
    * free (think "liberty")

2. What does the noun *liber, libri* mean?
    * book (think "library")
      N.B. You might give students the motto of St. John's College, Annapolis to translate here: *facio liberos ex liberis libris libraque* = I make free (citizens) out of children with books and a balance

3. What case is *Numine*?
    * ablative

4. What does the prefix *trans* of *transtulit* mean when it is a preposition?
    * across

5. What verb has *tuli* as the third principal part?
    * *fero, ferre, tuli, latum* = bear, carry, say, tell

p. 102

1. What verb gives us *esto*?
    *   *sum, esse, fui, futurus*

2. What case is *populi*?
    *   genitive

3. What gender is *lex*?
    *   feminine

4. What is the case and use of *scuto*?
    *   ablative of means

5. What person is *coronasti*?
    *   second singular perfect tense
        N.B. *coronasti* is short for *coronavisti*

p. 104

1. What person of the verb is *quaeris*?
    *   second singular

2. What grammatical form is *circumspice*?
    *   imperative

3. What does *circum* mean as a preposition?
    *   around

4. What case is *tyrannis*?
    *   dative

5. What case are *virtute* and *armis*?
    *   ablative

p. 108

1. Which motto on this page has an imperative?
    *   Iona College (*certa*)

2. Which motto has two hortatory subjunctives?
    *   University of Chicago (*crescat...excolatur*)

3. Which motto has an ablative object of a preposition?
    *   Princeton University (*sub Numine*)

4. Which motto has two third declension nouns?
    *   Duke University (*eruditio et religio*)

p. 110

1. What case is *scientia* when it is the object of *ex*?
    *   ablative

2. What case are *lux* and *veritas*?
    *   nominative

3. What mood is *fiat*?
    *   subjunctive (hortatory)

4. What grammatical form is *ministrare*?
    *   present active infinitive

5. What is *ministrari*?
    *   present passive infinitive

p. 112

1. What gender are *numen* and *lumen*?
    *   neuter

2. What grammatical form do *respice, adspice, prospice* represent?
    *   imperative singular

3. What tense is *irradient*?
    *   future

4. What case is *terras*?
    *   accusative direct object

p. 114

1. Find a future tense verb on this page.
   - liberabit

2. Find an imperative
   - festina

3. Find an adverb from a first/second declension adjective
   - lente

4. Find a present participle.
   - clamantis

5. Find three adverbs from third declension adjectives.
   - fortiter, feliciter, fideliter

p. 116

1. What present infinitive is on this page?
   - curare

2. What imperative is on this page?
   - descende

3. What two neuter accusatives are on this page?
   - facta, verba

4. What feminine accusative is on this page?
   - terram

p. 117

1. What is the Latin word for "faithful"?
   - fidelis

2. What is the Latin word for "always"?
   - semper

3. What is the Latin word for "or"?
   - aut

4. What is the Latin word for "now"?
   - nunc

5. What is the Latin word for "never"?
   - numquam

p. 118

1. What is the Latin word for "city"?
    *   urbs

2. Explain *fac* grammatically.
    *   irregular singular imperative
        N.B. The mnemonic "*Dic, duc, fac* and *fer*, look for the vowel it's not there!"
        is a good way to remember that there is no -e on the singular imperative
        of *fac*.

3. What is the grammatical form of *altius?*
    *   comparative adverb

4. What is the Latin word for "power"?
    *   potestas

5. Explain the grammatical form of *minimis...maximum.*
    *   superlative adjectives (*minimis* from *parvus* and *maximum* from *magnus*)

p. 120

1. What case is *me* in *noli me tangere?*
    *   accusative

2. What case are *mihi, Deo, regi, nobis, omnibus?*
    *   dative

3. What case are *vi* and *mente?*
    *   ablative

4. decline *vis*:
    *   vis, vis, vi, vim, vi
        vires, virium, viribus, viris, viribus

p. 121

1. What kind of verb are *morior* and *sequor*? Give their principal parts.
   - deponent:
   - *morior, mori, mortuus* = die
   - *sequor, sequi, secutus* = follow

2. Give the principal parts and present tense active of *volo, fio,* and *fero.*
   - *volo, velle, volui* = want, wish
     volo, vis, vult, volumus, vultis, volunt

   - *fio, fieri, factus* = become, be made, happen
     fio, fis, fit, fimus, fitis, fiunt

   - *fero, ferre, tuli, latum* = bear, carry, bring, say, tell
     fero, fers, fert, ferimus, fertis, ferunt

Abbreviations Questions for Latin Students:

N.B. It might be helpful to ask a student to write the whole phrase and its abbreviation on the board as you ask each question. That way everyone can see the Latin involved.

1. What gender is the Latin word *opus* in the expression *opus citatum?* (Hint: what does the ending of *citatum* tell you?)
    - neuter

2. Where is the Latin word we translate "and' in the expression *Senatus Populusque Romanus?*
    - The *-que* on the end of *Populus* means "and." A syllable attached to the end of a Latin word like this is called an enclitic, and it has no meaning by itself. Another common enclitic is *-ne* which makes a statement into a question. Enclitic comes from a Greek word which means "leaning on."

3. What do we call a verbal noun like *operandi* in the expression *modus operandi?*
    - a gerund

4. Why are *meridiem* in the expression *post meridiem* and *scriptum* in the expression *post scriptum* accusative?
    - the preposition *post* takes the accusative

5. Look at the list of abbreviations and find as many imperatives as possible:
    - confer, *nota* (in the expression *nota bene*), *vide* (in the expression *quod vide*), *recipe*

6. What case is *Domini* in *anno Domini,* *vitae* in the expression *curriculum vitae,* *exempli* in *exempli gratia?*
    - genitive (of the Lord, of life, of an example)

7. What part of speech is *statim?*
    - adverb

8. What gender and number are *alia* in the expression *et alia* and *cetera* in *et cetera?*
    - neuter plural

9. *Nil* in the expression *nil per os* is one way to write the Latin word for "nothing." What is the other?
    - nihil

10. What construction is illustrated in the expression *quod erat demonstrandum?*
    - periphrastic (gerundive + erat)

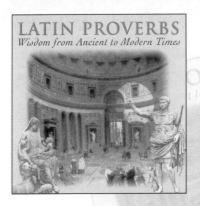

Hear the Sound of Latin

O Abies (Oh Christmas Tree)
Christmas Carols in Latin
C.C Couch & Teddy Irwin

The lyrics to the 12 carols sung in Classical and Ecclesiastical Latin can be found in *Latine Cantemus*.

It Came Upon The Midnight Clear • God Rest You Merry, Gentlemen • Jingle Bells • Deck The Halls • O Christmas Tree • We Wish You A Merry Christmas • Joy To The World • The First Noel • O Come All Ye Faithful • Silent Night • Hark The Herald Angels Sing • O Little Town Of Bethlehem

Running Time: 35:03 (2003) Audio CD, Order Number: 00001

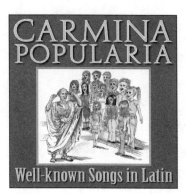

Carmina Polularia
Well-known Songs in Latin
C.C Couch & Teddy Irwin

The Latin lyrics to the 15 songs sung in Latin can be found in *Latine Cantemus*.

America the Beautiful • Oh, Susannah • Greensleeves • Old Folks at Home • Guantanamera • This Old Man • Old MacDonald • Gaudeamus Igitur • Row, Row, Row Your Boat • What Shall We Do with the Drunken Sailor • Polly Wolly Doodle • Shenandoah • Auld Lang Syne • My Bonnie • Oh, When the Saints Go Marching In

Running Time: 49:21 (2004) Audio CD, Order Number: 00003

Latine Cantemus
Cantica Popularia Latine Reddita
Franz Schlosser

Schlosser's translations of sixty popular songs along with forty-nine traditional songs form the largest compendium of Latin songs in print. Folk songs, ballads, popular songs, spirituals, Christmas carols, children's songs, and chanties fill this volume and will fill the hearts of those who sing them with enjoyment and delight. Appendices of Gregorian chants, Christmas songs, and traditional Latin favorites with the musical notation are included.

Illus., vii + 135 pp. (1996) Paperback, ISBN 0-86516-315-4

Bolchazy-Carducci Publishers, Inc.
www.bolchazy.com

INDISPENSABLE LATIN GRAMMARS

A NEW LATIN SYNTAX
E. C. Woodcock

This book gives an historical account of the chief Latin constructions, and gives teachers more information on each structure than the traditional grammar books. The Index of Passages Quoted is especially useful for teachers.

This is a necessary reference and an indispensable vademecum for teachers and advanced students.

xxiv + 267 pp. (1959, Reprint 1987) Paperback, ISBN 0-86516-126-7

NEW LATIN GRAMMAR
Charles E. Bennett

Syntax and grammar make sense in this reprint of Bennett's revised grammar from 1908. Still a highly regarded and widely used resource both in and out of the classroom, this volume should be on every teacher's reference shelf.

Features: • The essential facts of Latin grammar written in a clear, direct manner • Specific examples from primary sources • An introduction on the history and stages of development of the Latin language • Sections on prosody, the Roman calendar, Roman names and definitions, and figures of syntax and rhetoric • Indices of the sources of the illustrative samples and principal parts of the most important verbs • General index

xvi + 287 pp. (1908, Reprint 1995) Paperback, ISBN 0-86516-261-1

GILDERSLEEVE'S LATIN GRAMMAR
B. L. Gildersleeve & G. Lodge

The *Latin Grammar* by B. L. Gildersleeve and G. Lodge has become the *sine qua non* of Latin grammar books in print today. A standard reference work in the field of Latin grammar for over a century, this reprint remains at the top in its field today.

Features: • Every grammar topic is treated to its fullest extent • Sections on the alphabet, pronunciation, accentuation • Most complete treatment of syntax available • A section on prosody • An appendix on the calendar, weights, money, and names • Index of verbs • General index

613 pp. (1895, third edition, reprint with additions 2003)
Paperback, ISBN 0-86516-353-7
Hardbound, ISBN 0-86516-477-0

 BOLCHAZY-CARDUCCI PUBLISHERS, INC.
WWW.BOLCHAZY.COM

VERGIL'S STORY AND CICERO'S TIMES TOLD WITH HUMOR

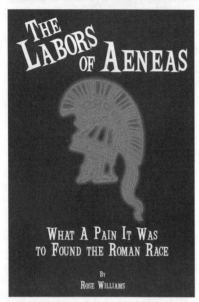

THE LABORS OF AENEAS
What A Pain It Was to Found the Roman Race
Rose Williams

The Labors of Aeneas is a delightful retelling of Vergil's *Aeneid* that has changed the tone, but not the tale. Ever-faithful to the story's facts, Rose Williams recounts Vergil's epic in a modern's voice—in witty, droll fashion. Readers with little or no classical background can savor the story, and easily follow a narrative renowned for its complexity. Those who already know the story will recognize, through tears of laughter, the unwitting narrator: the first-time reader, agape at the great cultural challenge this epic has always posed.

Features:
- the story of *The Aeneid*, Books I–XII
- black and white illustrations
- notes
- a glossary of gods prominent in *The Aeneid*

vi + 108 pp. (2003) 6" x 9" Paperback ISBN 0-86516-556-4

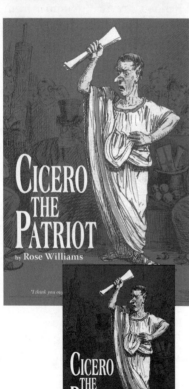

CICERO THE PATRIOT
Rose Williams

Light-hearted in tone but faithful to the facts, this readable volume interweaves the story of Cicero's private life and feelings with the development of his public life and his literary output. This book contains details and commentary on Cicero's speeches, letters, and philosophical writings and highlights the events in his world which served as background for some of the most poignant, as well as the most dramatic, writing ever done in Latin. Williams shows also the human side of the renowned orator and thereby allows the reader to savor Cicero's dreams, disappointments, and pursuits.

Students and teachers will enjoy this volume that helps to fill the gaps in their knowledge of Cicero. The ethical principles that propelled the orator to courageous and ultimately fatal undertakings are told with memorable twists of language that offer comic relief and enhance the appreciation for Cicero as a total person.

An extensive glossary explaining customs and practices such as *salutationes* and the *Lupercalia* along with a timeline of Cicero's major works and the events of his life make this book an invaluable resource for both students and teachers.

Features:
- Comprehensive description of the events of Cicero's life
- Significant presentation of the historical circumstances of Cicero's life
- A timeline of historical events and the publication of Cicero's works
- An explanation of terms necessary to know (e.g. *cursus honorum* – the steps on the political ladder in Cicero's time)
- A summary of Cicero's life in a one-page format
- Teacher's Manual available

Student Text: (2004) Paperback, ISBN 0-86516-587-4
Teacher's Manual: (2004) Paperback, ISBN 0-86516-588-2

BOLCHAZY-CARDUCCI PUBLISHERS, INC.
WWW.BOLCHAZY.COM